GOTTHOLD EPHRAIM LESSING

Gotthold Ephraim Lessing, born in Kamenz in Saxony in 1729, gave up studying theology to become a writer. His first significant play, *Miss Sara Sampson* (1755), already indicated his lifelong ambition to rid the stage of artificiality and introduce a measure of realism and contemporaneity. There followed *Minna von Barnhelm* (1767), thought of as the first true German comedy, *Emilia Galotti* (1772), a tragedy set amongst the middle classes, and *Nathan the Wise* (1779). He was also a journalist, a critic and, briefly, a dramaturg (probably the first person to hold such a post) at the Hamburg National Theatre, out of which came his most important writing about the theatre, the essays making up his *Hamburg Dramaturgy* (1767-8). He died in Braunschweig in 1781.

EDWARD KEMP

Edward Kemp is a writer, director and dramaturg. He has adapted Molière's *Le Malade Imaginaire* and *Dom Juan* for the West Yorkshire Playhouse, the medieval *Mysteries* for the RSC and BBC Radio, and W.G. Sebald's *The Emigrants* for BBC Radio. His adaptation of Faulkner's *As I Lay Dying* has been seen at the Young Vic in London, and in Louisiana and Los Angeles. His play about the Gunpowder Plot, *5/11*, premiered at Chichester Festival Theatre in 2005. Work with his own company, The Table Show, has played at the National Theatre in London, as well as in Edinburgh, Leeds, Budapest and Wellington, New Zealand. He has written over a dozen short opera libretti, including collaborations with Sally Beamish, Terry Davies, Agostin Fernandez and Alwynne Pritchard.

Other Titles in this Series

Gotthold Ephraim Lessing

NATHAN THE WISE

in a version by
EDWARD KEMP

NICK HERN BOOKS
London
www.nickhernbooks.co.uk

A Nick Hern Book

This translation of *Nathan the Wise* first published in Great Britain
as a paperback original in 2003 by Nick Hern Books Limited, The Glasshouse.
49a Goldhawk Road, London W12 8QP

Reprinted 2005, 2010, 2012 (twice)

Copyright in this translation © 2003 Edward Kemp

Edward Kemp has asserted his right to be identified as the translator of this
work

Cover photo: Clare Park

Typeset by Country Setting, Kingsdown, Kent CT14 8ES
Printed in the UK by Mimeo Ltd, Huntingdon, Cambridgeshire PE29 6XX

A CIP catalogue record for this book is available from the British Library

ISBN 978 1 85459 765 6

Gotthold Ephraim Lessing (1729–1781)

If there were ever to be a patron saint of dramaturgs then
Gotthold Ephraim Lessing wouldn't be a bad candidate. He
was German (a good start), held the post of literary adviser
during at least one of the many eighteenth-century attempts to
launch a German National Theatre and penned 'the first really
substantial German contribution to dramatic theory', which
was even called *Hamburgische Dramaturgie*. He discoursed
polemically on subjects from fine art to theology, qualified as a
medic and knew English, French, Spanish, Latin, Greek and
Hebrew. He wrote the first long-running German comedy, the
first bourgeois tragedy, and in *Nathan the Wise* created one of
the most significant dramatic works of the European Enlightenment. He was also an inveterate gambler, a keen horseman,
an enthusiastic dancer and quite capable of arguing one case
passionately today and the opposite just as fervently tomorrow.

Exactly how he'd take the idea of canonisation I'm not so sure.
The son of a Lutheran pastor (who was appalled when his son
abandoned his theological studies for the theatre, and not at all
appeased by young Gotthold's suggestion that he might become
the German Molière) Lessing's relationship to Christianity was
never straightforward. His final work, *The Education of the
Human Race* (which posits a kind of post-religious Christianity
of the kind favoured by much modern theology and presents
an individuated God a hundred and fifty years before Jung)
tellingly takes its epigraph from St Augustine: 'For the same
reasons this is all in a certain sense true and in a certain sense
false'. It seems to have been the narrow-minded superstition
of contemporary Christianity, exhibited in its slavish adherence
to a Bible that 'clearly contains more than is essential to
religion', which aroused his rationalist ire. But just as Nathan's
empiricism does not deny the existence of angels, so Lessing's
rationalism in no way excludes the spirit, nor did his intellectual relativism reject the possibility that there might in fact be
a definitive truth. 'Religion is not true because evangelists and

apostles taught it, but they taught it because it was true,' he argued in the course of the religious controversy that would eventually give birth to *Nathan*, and in his version of Boccaccio's story of the rings the possibility is held out that one day a judge might come who can tell us which of the three rings is the true one. But Lessing famously wrote that if God offered him the choice between the truth and the quest for the truth he would choose the latter. The truth is out there, says Lessing, he's just not entirely sure it's healthy for us to know it. Why? Because when we believe we have the truth we tend to do terrible things to other humans.

Lessing certainly knew what the Christian claim to the truth had done to the Jews in Germany even before the events of the twentieth century. A review of his early comedy *The Jews* described it as improbable because a Jew could not be upright and noble. In reply Lessing quoted a letter from his closest friend Moses Mendelssohn (grandfather of the composer), who was known as the 'German Socrates', was idolised and visited by intellectuals from all over Europe, yet entered Berlin through the Rosenthal Gate, the only one open to Jews and to cattle, and struggled all his life to gain any kind of legal status for himself and for his family. To Lessing his Jewish chess companion was living proof of one of the Enlightenment's major tenets: he had 'become what he was by the force of his *own* thinking, with the help of only a few books'. *Selbstdenken* – independent thinking for oneself – was always paramount to Lessing, he relished it in himself and sought to provoke it in others: 'I am not duty-bound to resolve the difficulties I create. May my ideas always be somewhat disjunct, or even appear to contradict one another, if only they are ideas in which readers will find material that stirs them to think for themselves'.

This wilfulness may go someway to explain the extraordinary confection that is *Nathan the Wise* and which makes it quite unlike anything else Lessing wrote or anything else in the German theatrical canon. In part this uniqueness must have resulted from the play's need to use subterfuge to hide its unorthodox religious views. A dramatic fable set in a historical and oriental setting would not be subject to the same censorship as a polemical pamphlet. Lessing broke with his own and

contemporary convention by calling it neither a tragedy nor
a comedy, but 'a dramatic poem' and wrote it, unlike any of
his other completed plays, in verse. But the iambic pentameter
is so shot through with interruptions and run-on lines, exclam-
ations and elisions (not to mention Lessing's own system of
speech-based punctuation) that the pulse of the verse is often
hard to perceive. Nor does its poetry consist much in lyrical
outbursts but more in the symmetry of its construction, which
adds considerably to the sense of Providence at work; a pattern
of redemption whose closest kin at times seems to be the late
plays of Shakespeare.

It's well known that Lessing was one of the first great German
champions of Shakespeare. While theatrical orthodoxy held in
esteem the pale imitations of French classicism, it was Lessing
who pointed out that for all their flouting of Aristotelian
conventions *Romeo and Juliet, Hamlet* and *Othello* are greater
plays than the tragedies of Voltaire, and encouraged his com-
patriots to study Shakespeare. But unlike his followers it was
not the mixing of comedy and tragedy that appealed to Lessing,
indeed he argued against it, and though there's certainly a
Shakespearean mix in *Nathan*, the play as a whole tends
towards an Aristotelian unity of time, if not quite action and
place. What Lessing valued in Shakespeare was the power of
his psychological penetration. Once again, it was the human
and the personal that attracted this most polemical of writers.
And it is especially poignant therefore that this great work of
the Enlightenment should have at its core a human tragedy. In
1776 at the age of 47 he married Eva König, a widow to whom
he had been engaged for five years. A son was born on Christ-
mas day the following year, but he survived only a few hours,
Eva herself died shortly afterwards. 'My wife is dead,' Lessing
wrote to a friend, 'and so now I've had this experience too.
I'm glad there aren't many similar experiences left for me to
have'. For a man so determined to believe in the benevolent
design of the universe it must have been a bitter test.

Ten years after the end of the Nazi regime (under which both
Nathan the Wise and *The Jews* were banned) and at the height
of the Cold War, the German-born Jewish writer Hannah
Arendt selected Gotthold Lessing as one of her *Men in Dark*

Times. She noted how the theme of friendship runs through *Nathan the Wise*: 'this friendship is obviously so much more important to Lessing than the passion of love that he can brusquely cut the love story off short . . . and transform it into a relationship in which friendship is required and love ruled out'. She concludes that 'In the end Nathan's wisdom consists solely in his readiness to sacrifice truth to friendship'. Looking at her own age she considers 'Suppose that a race could indeed be shown, by indubitable scientific evidence to be inferior . . . *Would any such doctrine, however convincingly proved, be worth the sacrifice of so much as a single friendship between two men?* . . . Lessing would not have found any difficulty in answering the question. No insight into the nature of Islam or Judaism or of Christianity could have kept him from entering into a friendship with a convinced Mohammedan or a pious Jew or a believing Christian. Any doctrine that in principle barred the possibility of friendship between two human beings would have been rejected by his untrammelled and unerring conscience. He would instantly have taken the human side and given short shrift to the learned or unlearned discussion in either camp. That was Lessing's humanity'. Saint or no he is a man for these times.

A Note on This Version

Lessing never saw *Nathan the Wise* on stage. The text was
published by private subscription in 1779, two years before
his death, and it is quite possible that he never intended it for
performance. The first German production in 1783 was not
a success and the play at full stretch would certainly tax the
patience of most English audiences, lasting at least four and
a half hours (at a conservative estimate) and including a great
many passages where any sense of dramatic motive is capsized
under the weight of debate. It was not until 1801 when the
play was revived in a version by Schiller that Goethe
acclaimed it as a masterpiece and so sealed its place in the
German literary canon.

Schiller's version consists largely of some substantial pruning
of all the longer philosophical and theological exchanges, a
fairly brutal diminution of the female roles, especially Sittah,
and the removal of a jolly (if inconsequential) scene when
Saladin's gold arrives brought by three Emirs, only to be taken
away again by those same Emirs in the whirl of Saladin's
generosity. In addition Schiller adds two short speeches, one
for Al-Hafi explaining why he left the desert, and one for
Sittah at the opening of the 'ring' scene (Scene 6) clarifying
the way the 'trap' will work. In total these changes reduce
Lessing's original by about a sixth and reins it somewhere
within the four-hour mark.

In our quest to bring this immense text to theatrical life Schiller
proved an extremely useful guide, though we did not follow all
of his excisions: perhaps for reasons of censorship he removes
some of the more resolutely anti-Christian material, which we
have restored along with many of the cuts to the female roles
(Sittah is back almost to her full glory). But beyond Schiller's
trims and a few additional ones of our own the entire script has
undergone a process of 'compression'. The guiding principle
here has been to make Lessing's arguments immediate and

accessible to the audience on one hearing, as they must be in the theatre, and which I fear they seldom are in the original. I don't believe that as a result of this compression we have lost any substantial thought or idea, but the overall effect has been to enable us to make the play's dialectic more theatrically alive and more actively inhabited by the characters – and to make it a manageable evening in the theatre.

We have also for theatrical reasons restructured some of the second half of the play. In Lessing Al-Hafi has only three scenes, the final one being before Nathan goes off to meet Saladin (Scene 4): thus one of the most striking and loveable characters in the piece is gone before the midway point. This seemed both unsatisfactory and unfair, so we cut his original final scene in half and saved the second part of it until just before Nathan's real crisis point in Scene 10. In performance this seems to work very well, and I hope might have met with Lessing's approval since he was himself so fond of Al -Hafi that he planned a sequel called 'The Dervish'. Also in Scene 10 Lessing has the Friar go off to get the little book, returning with it a scene later, following a rather uneventful soliloquy from the Templar. We felt quite strongly that by this point the audience would require some kind of narrative drive towards the climax, and so have fused together these two scenes.

Otherwise my own additions are relatively few and far between. I have tried to clarify the historical background and in the process endeavoured to sharpen some of the connections between the Jerusalem of 1192 and the Middle East of 2003. Lessing's own volatility shows in the vertiginous mood swings he asks his characters to negotiate often in only a single line. These by and large I have not tampered with, and the Chichester company have proved they can be electrifying theatre. Elsewhere, notably in the scene between Rachel and the Templar (Scene 5) and the final reconciliation, the writing felt too bald to bold, especially with the ghost of Shakespeare loitering in the wings, so I have added a few minor flourishes of my own. The exquisite lightness of touch that can embrace both the joy and pain of human experience is entirely Lessing's, and while I am guilty of adding a few jokes here and there, in performance the best laughs have often been his.

The decision to put this version into prose rather than verse was taken early on in the process of translation. As I've written above, Lessing's verse is an unsettled and unsettling creature and the attempt to follow it seems to have undone many of my predecessors: what can seem questing and fraught in the German rapidly becoming circumlocutory, or just plain incomprehensible in English. In addition if it's the case, as has been argued, that Lessing used verse to put a 'fable-like' aura around the action, to distance it in some way behind a poetic scrim (perhaps further to hoodwink the censor) then this was the exact opposite of what we wanted to achieve, which was to expose and revivify the story in the light of contemporary events. However the play *is* a kind of fable (there is something very Arabian Nights not only about the setting and characters but also in the obsessive story-telling which infects almost every scene) and this required some kind of discreet heightening of form and language. The solution I came to was a simple reversal of the components in Lessing's own mix. Whereas he had the written the play in a verse that reads more like prose I have translated it into prose that is to a large extent more like verse. Large stretches of my version are in the form of 'buried' iambic, that is they have the pulse of iambic meter, but of an entirely irregular line length. I suggest there is no need whatsoever for the actors to draw attention to this in performance – it is simply a kind of invisible glue which binds the text together.

Finally I must acknowledge the immense debt I owe to Steven Pimlott, who asked me to translate the play in the first place and whose wisdom, intelligence and boundless enthusiasm was invaluable both in helping to shape the text and then in bringing it to life in the theatre. I would also like to pay thanks to the original Chichester cast, who all contributed at the very least a more telling word or neater turn of phrase to this script, and to the Assistant Director Lucy Jameson who proved a tireless guardian of Lessing's work when I was in the rehearsal room and of mine when I was not.

EDWARD KEMP
Chichester, May 2003

The first performance of this version was given on 26 April 2003 in the Minerva Theatre, Chichester, as part of the 2003 Chichester Festival Theatre season. The cast was as follows:

SALADIN	Jeffery Kissoon
SITTAH	Noma Dumezweni
NATHAN	Michael Feast
RACHEL	Kay Curram
DAYA	Darlene Johnson
THE TEMPLAR	Geoffrey Streatfeild
AL-HAFI	Jonathan Cullen
THE PATRIARCH	Alfred Burke
THE LAY BROTHER	Steven Beard

Director Steven Pimlott
Designer Antony McDonald
Lighting Designer Hugh Vanstone
Sound Designer Greg Clarke
Assistant Director Lucy Jameson
Costume Supervisor Gabrielle Dalton
Company Stage Manager Amelia Ferrand-Rock
Stage Manager Suzanne Bourke
Deputy Stage Manager Alastair Brain
Assistant Stage Manager Jessica Cutler

This version of *Nathan the Wise* was revived in a new production at Hampstead Theatre, London, on 19 September 2005. The cast was as follows:

SALADIN	Vincent Ebrahim
SITTAH	Shelley King
NATHAN	Michael Pennington
RACHEL	Celia Meiras
DAYA	Anna Carteret
THE TEMPLAR	Sam Troughton
AL-HAFI/THE PATRIARCH	Justin Avoth
THE LAY BROTHER	Ewart James Walters

Director Anthony Clark
Designer Patrick Connellan
Lighting Designer James Farncombe
Sound Designer Steven Brown
Assistant Director Dan Ayling
Costume Supervisor Mary Charlton
Casting Siobhan Bracke
Company Stage Manager Julie Issott
Deputy Stage Manager Lorna Seymour
Assistant Stage Manager Jo Oliver

NATHAN THE WISE

Characters

Yusuf Salah-al-Din (SALADIN), *the Sultan*

SITTAH, *his sister*

NATHAN, *a rich Jew*

RACHEL, *his daughter*

DAYA, *a Christian*

TEMPLAR, *a Knight Templar*

AL-HAFI, *a dervish*

Heraclius, *the* PATRIARCH *of Jerusalem*

Bonafides, *a lay-*BROTHER

Setting: Jerusalem, 1192

Introite nam et heic Dii sunt! – Gellius

('Enter, for here too there are gods')

One

The courtyard of Nathan's house. Morning.

NATHAN *arrives home.*

Enter DAYA.

DAYA. Nathan! At last. Thank God you're home

NATHAN. I am. And thanks to God. But why 'at last', Daya? Couldn't you wait for my return? Forgive me, but Babylon's 200 miles from Jerusalem and debt-collecting takes time

DAYA. If you knew how near you came to grief

NATHAN. There was a fire. I've heard. I don't think there's any more to be said

DAYA. And if we'd lost the house

NATHAN. then we'd have built another. Bigger and more luxurious

DAYA. And Rachel? What if she'd been burnt alive

NATHAN. no need for houses then. But she was not. No one's told me this. She's not. Daya. The child is not dead.

DAYA. Would I be standing here to tell you if she was?

NATHAN. Don't frighten me. You wicked Christian. My dear, dear Rachel

DAYA. your Rachel is she

NATHAN. I say she is. I have the greatest claim that any man could have: she was given to me by the good God himself

DAYA. in payment

NATHAN. in payment, yes, if you'll have it so, for my suffering

DAYA. and now you make me suffer in return

NATHAN. What are you muttering

DAYA. nothing

NATHAN. good.

DAYA. But one day

NATHAN. Wait, I'd forgotten, I've something to show you

DAYA. one day when my conscience

NATHAN. just look at what I bought in Babylon. For you.
You'll not find its like anywhere. I've not given even
Rachel finer. What d'you say?

DAYA. I say you never change, Nathan. Everything's made
better with a gift

NATHAN. so take the gift and then we're friends again.

DAYA. You are the kindest, best-hearted man I know and yet

NATHAN. I am a Jew. Strange isn't it

DAYA. You know what I was going to say

NATHAN. then you have no need to say it

DAYA. and so who will speak for you on the day that God
exacts his vengeance?

NATHAN. I don't know. We'll have to see. Maybe I can give
him something too.

But where is she, Daya? Why's she not come to greet me?

DAYA. You'll have to ask her yourself. I can get no sense from
her. She's so nervy now, sees fires everywhere. When she
sleeps her mind's a fervour, but when she wakes – not there
at all

NATHAN. poor child. She has had a shock

DAYA. This morning I couldn't wake her. I thought she was
dead. Then suddenly up she sits: 'Listen! My father's
camels!' I couldn't hear a thing. 'There! His voice!' Then
closes her eyes and falls back on the pillow. I ran straight
down and here you were. She thinks of nothing but you.
Well, apart from him

NATHAN. Him?

DAYA. The man who rescued her

NATHAN. she was rescued? Who by?

DAYA. A young Knight Templar

NATHAN. a Templar? Are you sure?

DAYA. They're not easily mistaken

NATHAN. no. But a Templar in Jerusalem. Alive.

DAYA. He was a prisoner. The Sultan pardoned him

NATHAN. By God. Saladin pardon a Templar? Now I don't
know which was the miracle, her escape or his

DAYA. and if he hadn't thrown himself into the fire, risked the
life he'd just regained, she'd be lost to us now.

NATHAN. But where is he, Daya? I must speak to him, thank
him. Reward him. You explained my absence, I hope,
promised him something when I returned

DAYA. how could I? No one knew where he came from.
He was suddenly there. We'd never seen him near the
house, he can have had no idea where he was going, but he
dives into the fire, his white cloak wrapped about his face
following the sound of her screams. I thought he was gone,
dead, they both were. You could see nothing in the smoke.
And then there he is again, carrying her in his arms. We're
cheering, crying, shouting, and he's cold, like a statue. Lays
her on the ground, pushes his way past us and disappears

NATHAN. he can't have vanished

DAYA. A few days later we found him. In the palm-grove. He
paces up and down beside the tomb of Our Risen Lord. We
were overjoyed. I raced out to meet him, thanked him,
praised his courage. I said 'Come and see her. She won't be
at peace until she has thanked you herself.' I begged him

NATHAN. but

DAYA. would he listen? No, he mocked me, ridiculed me,
humiliated me

NATHAN. and thus deterred

DAYA. you know me better than that. I've been back every day, and every day the same. What I haven't suffered from that man. And would gladly suffer again for her. But he stopped coming to the Holy Sepulchre, and no one knows where he's gone. What are you thinking?

NATHAN. I'm trying to put myself in Rachel's position. One moment this man behaves like a hero, I worship him, the next my idol treats me like a dog. If I'm Rachel by now I've turned myself into the heroine of a tragic love story. Am I right?

DAYA. What d'you expect? She's a girl. They're only harmless fantasies

NATHAN. Are they?

DAYA. Her best is that he wasn't a real Templar at all, but an angel. You know since she was a child she's imagined angels watching over her. This one emerged from his shimmering cloud into the earthly form of a Templar in the heart of the fire. Don't smile. You know there's not a Jew, Christian or Muslim who doesn't secretly believe in angels

NATHAN. and I include myself. Go and see if she's awake yet. I'd like to speak to her. Then I shall seek out our rogue angel myself and entice him down to earth with us

DAYA. good luck

NATHAN. and when she meets him in the flesh, Daya, I think you'll find that, like any woman, she's happy that he's not an angel, but a man.

DAYA. For a good person, you are very wicked.

Enter RACHEL.

RACHEL. Father. Is it really you? I thought I must have dreamt your voice. Well? What mountains and rivers lie between us now? Here we stand breathing the same air and you don't rush to embrace me. I was in a fire. I nearly died. Don't tremble. It was only nearly. Fire is a terrible way to die

NATHAN. my child, my darling child

RACHEL. You had to cross the Euphrates, the Tigris, the Jordan – all those rivers – I used to worry about you so much before the fire came. But now I think how wonderful it must be to die in water, how cooling, how welcoming. No, you're not drowned and I'm not burnt. We should rejoice and praise God. He bore you over the waters on the wings of invisible angels. But I saw my angel, he carried me out of the fire on his white wings

NATHAN. he had wings

RACHEL. I saw them. I saw him as plainly as I see you

NATHAN. and my daughter must have seemed as beautiful to him as he did to her

RACHEL. who are you trying to flatter, the angel or yourself, my father?

NATHAN. But let's suppose only for a moment that there was no angel. Let's suppose it was a man. Wouldn't a man have *seemed* like an angel because he saved you?

RACHEL. But he didn't *seem* like an angel, he was one

NATHAN. Rachel

RACHEL. Who taught me that angels exist? That they hover around us at all times? And that God sends them to work miracles for those who love Him. And I've loved Him haven't I?

NATHAN. You have and He loves you. And isn't it miracle enough that my Rachel owes her life to a man whose own life was saved by a miracle? When did anyone hear of Saladin pardoning a Templar? Or for that matter of a Templar seeking Saladin's pardon

RACHEL. But that proves it, don't you see. It couldn't possibly have been a real Templar, because what could a Templar be doing in Jerusalem? He only *seemed* to be one, but actually he was an angel.

NATHAN. That's good, very good.

Daya, your turn. You're the one who told me he was a
prisoner. What else do you know?

DAYA. About him? Only what people say

NATHAN. which is?

DAYA. The Sultan pardoned him because he looked so like a
favourite brother apparently. I don't know his name, but he
died twenty years ago and they never found the body. That's
what they say, if you want to believe them

NATHAN. and you don't

DAYA. He's Saladin

NATHAN. and so incapable of affection? Even you'll admit he
loves his family. Why shouldn't he have had a brother he
loved more than the rest? And as for the resemblance –
well, almost every week you tell me you've seen someone
who reminds you of a friend in Switzerland, and then some
great story follows of how much you miss your homeland

DAYA. It still doesn't make any sense

NATHAN. why? Because there aren't any angels involved?

DAYA. Why should Saladin pardon a Templar

RACHEL. and how could a Templar vanish into thin air?

NATHAN. When you say vanish do you mean why has he
stopped pacing up and down in the palm-grove outside our
house? Or have you scoured the city for him?

DAYA. Of course we haven't

NATHAN. So how do you know he is not lying somewhere
injured

RACHEL. injured

DAYA. because I know he's not

NATHAN. or, God forbid, sick. Consider – he's a European,
not used to the climate here. The heat of the day, the
freezing nights

RACHEL. he's sick. I know it

DAYA. no, he's not. Your father is just supposing

NATHAN. imagine him lost in a strange land. No friends

RACHEL. but where is he? Where?

DAYA. Nathan

NATHAN. no one to come to his aid. Nothing to console him but the thought of his one good deed

DAYA. stop it, you're hurting her.

NATHAN. throwing himself into the flames for a girl he'd never met

DAYA. you'll kill her if you carry on like this

NATHAN. and that's how you could have killed him with your harmless fantasies.

Rachel, Rachel, this is medicine, not poison. He lives. He is not sick. He is quite well

RACHEL. are you sure?

NATHAN. I'm sure

RACHEL. how d'you know?

NATHAN. because God rewards the good we do on earth on earth as well. And you must learn this: dreams are easy, deeds are hard. Imagine angels all you like but let them inspire you to action, not distract you from it.

RACHEL. Please don't leave me on my own again

NATHAN. You're not alone. You have Daya

There's a Muslim out there eyeing up my camels. Do either of you know him?

DAYA. That's your dervish

NATHAN. No

DAYA. it is. Your chess companion

NATHAN. Al-Hafi? But look at what he's wearing

DAYA. He's got a job. He's the Sultan's Treasurer now

NATHAN. have you gone mad? Al-Hafi?

> But he's coming in. Indoors with you both. Vanish.

> DAYA *and* RACHEL *go*.

> *Enter* AL-HAFI *in official robes*.

AL-HAFI. Go on, feast your eyes!

NATHAN. I'm wondering who it is. Do I know any dervishes who dress so splendidly?

AL-HAFI. Can a dervish hold no place in the world?

NATHAN. I thought the place of the true dervish was outside the world

AL-HAFI. then by the Prophet maybe I'm no true dervish. But when one is compelled

NATHAN. Compelled? How does one compel a dervish?

AL-HAFI. You ask him to do something he believes will benefit people

NATHAN. then by our mutual God, embrace me and welcome to the world.

AL-HAFI. You might first want to ask what my new position in the world is

NATHAN. I can't think I care

AL-HAFI. even if it might make our friendship awkward for you?

NATHAN. I'll risk it – if at heart you're still a dervish. And besides it's good to see you dressed for a change.

AL-HAFI. These are my official robes

NATHAN. if you say so.

AL-HAFI. Then tell me, great Nathan: if you were Sultan, what post could I expect at your court?

NATHAN. that's easy. You'd be my dervish.

> Alright, if you must – my cook

AL-HAFI. cook

NATHAN. you'd be a good cook

AL-HAFI. why not footman while you're about it? Call yourself a friend. The real Sultan knows me better. He's appointed me his treasurer

NATHAN. you? He's let a dervish loose in his accounts

AL-HAFI. only the household. His father controls the Exchequer

NATHAN. but still the Sultan's household is not small

AL-HAFI. not when every beggar in the city belongs to it

NATHAN. I thought Saladin hated beggars

AL-HAFI. he does. So he's buying them off the streets. And at such a rate he'll be a beggar himself before long.

What d'you say, my friend? Have I made a mistake?

NATHAN. I don't know – what does he pay you?

AL-HAFI. Me – not much. But to you he could be very profitable

NATHAN. how so?

AL-HAFI. Because there's a caravan of gold coming from Egypt tomorrow. It's been coming tomorrow since the day I took the job. And in the meantime he's run up debts like there is no tomorrow. So if you offered to tide him over, you could charge him what interest you liked until tomorrow comes

NATHAN. and interest on the interest

AL-HAFI. of course

NATHAN. and interest on that interest

AL-HAFI. naturally

NATHAN. and interest on the interest on that interest

AL-HAFI. why not?

NATHAN. until all my capital has been turned to interest? Al-Hafi, I'm not interested.

AL-HAFI. Oh dear. Then we'd best not see each other again.

NATHAN. Why?

AL-HAFI. Because I was counting on you

NATHAN. to do what?

AL-HAFI. To get me through this job with honour. Your purse has never been closed to me before

NATHAN. My friend, let's understand each other. To Al-Hafi the dervish I would give everything I own. But to Al-Hafi, the keeper of Saladin's household accounts

AL-HAFI. Kind as you're shrewd and shrewd as you're wise. As I feared. But trust me, my friend, before these robes have faded, I'll leave them hanging on a peg here in Jerusalem and I'll be barefoot beside the Ganges with my teachers

NATHAN. that's the Al-Hafi I know

AL-HAFI. and playing chess with them

NATHAN. what else? But whatever possessed you to become his treasurer?

AL-HAFI. What tempted me you mean.

In the desert I would sit while wise elders told me how the world was going to the bad because it lacked honest minds. No wonder, I thought, because we're all sitting here in the desert talking about it. But if it's so simple to prevent evil, as they taught, and so easy to promote good, as they taught, shouldn't we do something. And so I came to this city, I watched, I learnt, I took a job.

NATHAN. A job yes, but with Saladin

AL-HAFI. He flattered me. For the first time in my life, I was flattered

NATHAN. how?

AL-HAFI. 'Only one who has begged knows what beggars need. Only one who has begged knows how beggars should be best supported.' The last treasurer was too cold for his liking. He was stingy and didn't smile enough with it. 'Al-Hafi will be different. When Al-Hafi is in charge Saladin will not only be generous, he will be seen to be generous too. Because Al-Hafi thinks like me, Al-Hafi understands like me.' The hypocrite

NATHAN. careful, my friend

AL-HAFI. What would you call it then? To oppress a hundred thousand, starve them, rob them, torture them, murder them and then play the philanthropist to one or two? And that's not all

NATHAN. it is enough

AL-HAFI. no, you see, I'm as bad. He corrupts, and I seek the glimmer of goodness in his corruption. And because of this tiny gleam I lend to his corruption my good name. Isn't that as hypocritical? Worse? Well?

NATHAN. Al-Hafi, go back to the desert as soon as you can. Amongst men I fear you'll soon forget to be a man

AL-HAFI. and so do I. Goodbye

NATHAN. what? No. I want to talk to you. The desert will wait. Al-Hafi

    AL-HAFI *goes*.

    I wanted to ask him about the Templar.

    Enter DAYA.

DAYA. Nathan

NATHAN. yes

DAYA. he's back

NATHAN. who?

DAYA. Him

NATHAN. the angel?

DAYA. In the palm-grove. He's eating dates

NATHAN. what, like a man

DAYA. please. She wants you to go and see him. But you'll need to hurry.

NATHAN. Now? I can't, I'm not

You must go. Tell him I've returned. Tell him Rachel's father is home now and that he is most welcome

DAYA. No point, Nathan. He's not going to come. He won't visit a Jew.

NATHAN. Then try to keep him there. Or see where he goes to. I'll be out as soon as I can.

NATHAN *goes indoors,* DAYA *leaves the house.*

Two

A palm grove between Nathan's house and the Holy Sepulchre.

The TEMPLAR *paces back and forth. The Lay-*BROTHER *is at some distance, as if wanting to speak to him.*

TEMPLAR. Good brother – or should I say father

BROTHER. no, brother is correct. Lay-brother

TEMPLAR. I wish I'd something to give you, but God knows I've nothing

BROTHER. thank you and may God reward your intent, but I was not sent out here to ask you for alms

TEMPLAR. I see. But you were sent

BROTHER. yes, from the cloister (here)

TEMPLAR. the same cloister where they just refused me the pilgrim's ration

BROTHER. indeed, but if you'd care to return with me now

TEMPLAR. thanks, but it's so long since I've eaten meat I don't know if I could stomach it. And these dates are going down a treat.

Why were you sent?

BROTHER. To get to know you. To find out what sort of man you are

TEMPLAR. I see. And who's interested – not you, I'd guess

BROTHER. the Patriarch, I imagine. It was his instruction

TEMPLAR. Then you can tell the Patriarch I'm a Knight Templar and I was taken prisoner in the attack on Tebnin. Twenty of the Order were brought here, and only one of us was pardoned by Saladin. So, now the Patriarch knows all he needs. More probably

BROTHER. though no more than he knew already. What he would like to know is what it means that Saladin pardoned you – and you alone

TEMPLAR. d'you think I know the answer? I'm on my knees, neck bared, awaiting the blow, when Saladin's eyes fix on me. He rushes to my side. I'm stood up, my hands are untied – I'm about to thank him – he's crying. He says nothing, I say nothing. He goes, I'm left.

What it means, the Patriarch must work out for himself.

BROTHER. He concludes from this that God has marked you out for great things

TEMPLAR. like what? Escorting pilgrims to Mount Sinai? Saving Jewish girls from housefires

BROTHER. it will become clear. Maybe the Patriarch himself has a task which is out of the ordinary

TEMPLAR. he does? Go on:

BROTHER. The Patriarch has determined the location of a fortress in Lebanon where Saladin's father is accumulating the sums necessary to finance the forthcoming conflict. Saladin is known to visit this fortress from time to time, travelling at night by isolated roads with little escort. Do you follow

TEMPLAR. never better

BROTHER. it would be easy to overpower him and put an end to his journey

TEMPLAR. and the Patriarch thought I would be the man to do this?

You should remind the Patriarch that I've sworn allegiance to a sacred and monastic rule, pledged to fight and die in the service of our Lord Jesus Christ.

BROTHER. Exactly, such a sacrifice would, in the eyes of God, be worthy of a most particular reward in Heaven

TEMPLAR. Were you listening when I told you what Saladin had done for me?

BROTHER. I was

TEMPLAR. but still you think

BROTHER. the Patriarch believes that the whole fate of Christendom hangs upon this deed, that God and your Order

TEMPLAR. should sanctify butchery

BROTHER. indeed not, but what is 'butchery' in the eyes of men may not, says the Patriarch, appear so to God

TEMPLAR. and you believe God wishes me to murder the man who spared my life

BROTHER. Saladin remains an enemy to Christendom and can never be your friend

TEMPLAR. so instead I should stab him in the back.

BROTHER. The Patriarch sympathises with your emotion, but gratitude, the Patriarch believes, is only due when the deed was directed at us personally. In your case it is said that you were pardoned simply because you reminded Saladin of his brother, not for any virtue of your own

TEMPLAR. Get out of here. Get out of here or I'll lose my temper with you. Go

BROTHER. Forgive me, sir. These were simply the Patriarch's instructions.

Goes.

DAYA *approaches*.

TEMPLAR. Oh, splendid. We've a saying in Swabia: devils always come in pairs.

DAYA. I've been looking for you everywhere. Thank God, sir, thank God. Where've you been all this time? You've not been sick

TEMPLAR. no

DAYA. you're quite well

TEMPLAR. yes

DAYA. because we've all been so worried

TEMPLAR. have you.

DAYA. You've been away

TEMPLAR. it would seem so

DAYA. when did you get back

TEMPLAR. yesterday

DAYA. our Rachel's father's returned too. Today. From Babylon. So perhaps now Rachel can look forward to

TEMPLAR. What?

DAYA. What we've asked you so often. And now her father's there to welcome you. He urges you to call whenever you like. He's come home with twenty camels laden with spices, gems, fabrics, the best you'll find in India, Persia, Syria, China

TEMPLAR. There's nothing I need.

DAYA. Do you know his people treat him like royalty? Though why they call him Nathan the Wise rather than Nathan the Rich I've never understood

TEMPLAR. perhaps to his people 'rich' and 'wise' are the same thing

DAYA. what they ought to call him is Nathan the Good. If he wasn't a good man d'you think I'd have stayed with him?

Or do you think I'd forgotten my proper worth as a
Christian? If I'd known that I was going to follow my late
husband to Palestine and there raise up a little Jewish girl.

Did I tell you about my husband? He was a good Christian.
He served in the Emperor Friedrich's army

TEMPLAR. he came from Switzerland and had the great
privilege to be drowned in the same river with the Emperor.
Why do you keep on pestering me?

DAYA. Sweet Jesus! Me, pester

TEMPLAR. yes. Listen. I don't want to see you ever again. Or
hear you. Or ever to be reminded of a deed which I did
without thinking, and when I think about it now, seems to
me utterly without reason. I don't regret it, but if it
happened again, it'd be your fault if I didn't ask a few
questions first, and maybe let what's burning burn.

DAYA. God forbid

TEMPLAR. So if you want to do something for me, I suggest
you never set eyes on me again. And for God's sake don't
send her father. A Jew's a Jew. In Swabia we speak as we
find. Look, I've wiped the girl's image from my memory –
if it was ever there

DAYA. but she's not forgotten yours

TEMPLAR. why? What's she expecting to happen?

DAYA. I. Who knows?

People aren't always what they seem to be

TEMPLAR. they're seldom better.

DAYA. No! Don't run off

TEMPLAR. Woman, this grove has been my only refuge in
this cursed city, but if I stay any longer, you will make me
hate it.

He goes.

DAYA. German bear.

Three

The Sultan's Palace.

SALADIN *and* SITTAH *playing chess.*

SITTAH. Where's your head today, Saladin? Not at chess, that's clear.

SALADIN. I give up, Sittah. You win. Tell Al-Hafi to give you the money. Where is he? I thought I called him.

Why do we have to play with these faceless pieces? I know, I know, because it is written, but I'm not playing with an Imam and I can never tell which is which. When the Lionheart and I play together we shall

No, it's not the pieces, Sittah. You're too calm, too quick and I'm

SITTAH. Dear brother, when are we ever going to be able to play properly again?

SALADIN. You think this is about the jihad? No.

But it wasn't me who broke the truce. I was ready to extend it. I long to see my little sister matched to a good husband. And Richard's brother would have been a good husband

SITTAH. naturally, because he's Richard's brother. And everything about the Lionheart is perfect

SALADIN. and Malek would have married Richard's sister and together we would have shaped the greatest family upon earth. You see, I like to think I'm worthy of my friends. We would have been the pillars of the world.

SITTAH. Dreams, brother. Of honourable Christians who behave like men. When will you learn they're Christians first and only men after? Their prophet was a good enough man, if for once they'd copy his goodness, instead of blindly following his name. But in the name of Christ they'll defame and destroy every other good man who ever lived

SALADIN. you mean in the name of Christ they required you and Malek to convert

SITTAH. because of course I couldn't love my husband if I weren't a Christian, because apparently the Most Merciful Creator neglected to give Muslims hearts.

SALADIN. But this demand was not made by the Christians

SITTAH. not the Lionheart, of course

SALADIN. it was the Templars

SITTAH. and aren't they Christians any longer

SALADIN. not in this. The Templars want to keep Acre

SITTAH. which they bought with the blood of three thousand Muslim prisoners

SALADIN. and which the treaty would have given us. It is the old Templar game. To protect their military interest, they advance their religious status, make themselves the arbiters of all that's sacred, answerable only to their Order and the Pope. Then having wrecked the treaty they're soldiers again and attack Tebnin before the truce is even cold. But soldiers or monks they can still die like men.

SITTAH. But if it's not the truce, what is gnawing at you?

SALADIN. What never ceases to? I've been in Lebanon with our father. He is despairing

SITTAH. What can we do? What does he need?

SALADIN. The one thing I cannot bring myself to name. Money. When we have it, it seems an encumbrance, when we lack it, indispensable.

Enter AL-HAFI.

SALADIN. And to speak of the devil. We've been calling for you

AL-HAFI. It's the gold from Egypt, isn't it?

SALADIN. It's come! Where is it?

AL-HAFI. I thought you had it. I thought that was why you'd sent for me

SALADIN. no.

AL-HAFI. So it didn't come today?

SALADIN. You're the Treasurer

AL-HAFI. oh dear.

SALADIN. It will come. It is coming. Tomorrow. And in the meantime you owe Sittah a thousand dinars

AL-HAFI. But

SALADIN. I'm not interested.

AL-HAFI. You lost again, I take it. And to Sittah. Always to Sittah

SITTAH. Is there something wrong with that?

AL-HAFI. You know as well as I do.

SITTAH *signals to him to keep quiet.*

AL-HAFI. Is this the game? You were white?

SITTAH. Yusuf, tell him I can have my money

AL-HAFI. oh you'll get it. Like you always do. His move?

SITTAH*(sotto voce)*. Are you mad?

AL-HAFI. But the game's not over

SALADIN. pay her

AL-HAFI. you see your Queen

SALADIN. there's nothing I can do with her

SITTAH. give me my money

AL-HAFI. a moment. Maybe your Queen's cornered, but you're still not in mate

SALADIN. I am

AL-HAFI. no, no, all you

SALADIN. I am because I want to be.

SALADIN *throws the board on the floor.*

AL-HAFI. Well, throw your money away, why don't you. As if you had any.

SALADIN. What's he saying?

SITTAH. You know Al-Hafi, always wants to be the centre of attention. And he loves to see me beg. But he always pays in the end, don't you?

AL-HAFI. No. I won't play this farce any longer. He must know the truth.

SALADIN. Who? What?

SITTAH. Al-Hafi, you promised me

AL-HAFI. I never expected it would go this far

SALADIN. What must I know?

SITTAH. It's nothing, brother. Don't let it bother you.

SALADIN. Sittah.

SITTAH. Alright. You know I'm always beating you at chess

SALADIN. not

SITTAH. yes, I am. But I don't need the money, not at the moment, where as you

So I said 'Al-Hafi, leave the money where it is'. But don't think you're keeping it – or Al-Hafi is. It's just a loan that's all.

AL-HAFI. I wish it was all.

SALADIN. What else is there? Tell me.

AL-HAFI. While we've been waiting for these caravans loaded with gold to appear from Egypt, she has

SITTAH. don't listen to him, brother

AL-HAFI. not only has she not taken anything but

SALADIN. You wonderful girl. You've been paying me out of your account, haven't you?

AL-HAFI. She's been supporting the entire household, and covering all your personal expenses.

SALADIN (*embracing her*). My dear little sister.

SITTAH. But brother, it was you who made me rich enough to do it in the first place

AL-HAFI. and who will in due course leave her as poor as himself

SALADIN. Poor? How can I be poor and have such a sister? When have I had more than I have now? When have I needed less? The shirt on my back, a sword, a horse – and God. What more do I need? These will never fail me. And yet Al-Hafi, I could be angry with you

SITTAH. brother, let's leave this

SALADIN. no. Surely there was someone else you could turn to before Sittah?

SITTAH. D'you think I would let anyone else have the privilege of lending to you? I won't. Not until you've taken my last dinar

AL-HAFI. which won't be long now.

SALADIN. Then Al-Hafi, it's down to you. You must borrow what you can, from whomever you can and at whatever price

AL-HAFI. Any suggestions where I might start?

SITTAH. What about your friend? I hear he's returned from Babylon.

AL-HAFI. My friend? Who's that?

SITTAH. The Jew whose praises you were singing the other day

AL-HAFI. a Jew? Praised by me?

SITTAH. 'To whom God,' – I think I can remember the exact words you used – 'To whom his God has given a lion's share of both the best and worst of good things'

AL-HAFI. are you sure I said that? I've no idea what it means

SITTAH. the worst is riches, the best wisdom

AL-HAFI. and you're sure I said that about a Jew?

SITTAH. About your friend Nathan.

AL-HAFI. Oh Nathan. Of course, I hadn't thought. And he's home is he? Well, it's true, he's not badly off. They don't call him 'The Wise' for nothing. Or 'The Rich'.

SITTAH. 'The Rich' they call him more than ever. The whole city's a-buzz with the treasures he's brought home. You should pay him a visit

AL-HAFI. to borrow money? From Nathan? No, no, no, no, no, no, no. That's why he's so wise: he never lends money to anybody

SITTAH. that's not the impression you gave me before

AL-HAFI. I may have said that in a crisis he'll lend stock, merchandise, gifts in kind. But money? Never. He's not altogether like other Jews. He's broad-minded, lives life to the full, plays a mean game of chess. He's a loyal friend in bad times as well as good. But by the Prophet, don't expect to see the inside of his purse

SITTAH. not even to allow Saladin to support his good causes

AL-HAFI. not even then.

SALADIN. Why've I never heard of this man before?

AL-HAFI. There are other doors I would much sooner knock upon than Nathan's. And I think I remember a Moor who is very well off, but always greedy for a little bit extra – I might just be able to catch him before

SITTAH. Wait, I haven't

SALADIN. Let him go.

AL-HAFI *gone*.

SITTAH. What d'you think that was about? Has his Jew deceived him, or's he trying to deceive us?

SALADIN. Since I haven't the first idea who the two of you
were discussing

SITTAH. all you need to know about him is he's got money

SALADIN. which I'll not have taken from him by force

SITTAH. depends what you mean by force. Putting a knife to
his throat? Burning his house down? No. He may be wise,
but he will have a weakness. We need to find it, and then
exploit it. And I think I know where it might lie.

Do you want to help our father or not? Then come with me.

Four

Outside Nathan's house, adjacent to the palm grove.

NATHAN *comes out with* RACHEL.

RACHEL. What took you so long? He'll be gone by now.

NATHAN. If he's left the palm-grove then we'll find him
somewhere else.

Look, there's Daya coming back now

RACHEL. she's lost him then

NATHAN. you don't know that

RACHEL. then why's she walking so slowly?

NATHAN. Rachel, calm down

RACHEL. Is that what you want? A daughter who is always
calm. Indifferent to the well-being of the man who saved
my life?

NATHAN. I've never asked you to be other than you are.
Though I think it's more than his well-being that's got you
so heated

RACHEL. What do you mean?

NATHAN. There's nothing to be ashamed of. It's nature. Only promise me you'll not hide your feelings from me – whatever you decide.

Enter DAYA.

NATHAN. So?

DAYA. He's pacing again. Up and down under the palm-trees.

RACHEL. Did you speak to him?

NATHAN. I should talk to him alone. You two go inside.

RACHEL. I want to see him close up

NATHAN. not yet. Look, he's coming this way. Quick, inside

DAYA. come on. There's a window on the roof where we can

RACHEL. I know.

DAYA *and* RACHEL *go inside*.

Enter TEMPLAR.

NATHAN. Excuse me, sir

TEMPLAR. What?

NATHAN. If you wouldn't mind

TEMPLAR. What is it, Jew?

NATHAN. I'd like to talk

TEMPLAR. Can I prevent you?

NATHAN. Please. I am forever in your debt

TEMPLAR. ah. Then I think

NATHAN. My name is Nathan and the girl you saved is my daughter. I want

TEMPLAR. to thank me? Save your breath. I've endured sufficient thanks already. And besides I didn't save her because she was your daughter. It was my duty as a Templar. And at that moment my life had become a burden to me, so I was overjoyed to gamble it for someone else's – even if that someone did turn out to be a Jew.

NATHAN. So gallant and so full of hate. And though you wouldn't be the first, there's no need to make yourself a demon just to shield yourself from praise. What do you want then? Forgive me, but you are a prisoner in a foreign land and I'm sure there must be something I can do to help.

TEMPLAR. You? I don't think so

NATHAN. I am a rich man

TEMPLAR. I never met a Jew who was the better for being rich

NATHAN. so why not exploit him for his riches

TEMPLAR. if you insist. Then I accept your offer on behalf of my uniform. When it's gone beyond repair, I'll look you up and you can lend me the money for a new one. Don't look so disappointed. There's life in the old thing yet. See, just this one mark upon the cloak.

NATHAN *looks at the cloak.*

TEMPLAR. It's singed.

Must have been while I was carrying your daughter.

NATHAN. Strange that a cloak should be more eloquent of a man's worth than his own words.

Oh, please, forgive me

TEMPLAR. What?

NATHAN. A tear. It fell on

TEMPLAR. please. It doesn't matter. It's seen worse.

NATHAN. Might I borrow this?

TEMPLAR. Why?

NATHAN. I should like to show it to my daughter very much

TEMPLAR. why so?

NATHAN. To let her kiss it. She longs to offer you her heartfelt thanks for what you did. But now I see that she must yearn in vain.

TEMPLAR. Jew – Nathan you said your name was? – I should
explain

NATHAN. I understand. There she was, an excitable young
woman, a servant all too eager to be of service and a father
far from home. You were afraid, I think.

You feared temptation, you feared you could not master it.
And for that I thank you.

TEMPLAR. And I must confess you recognize the way a
Templar's trained to think

NATHAN. why only Templars? And why do they need this
training? I recognize how good people think, and how good
people act no matter where they come from

TEMPLAR. you think that all good people are the same

NATHAN. they wear different clothes, and come in many
shapes and colours

TEMPLAR. and are there more here than other lands

NATHAN. about the same.

Great men wherever require a lot of space: you plant too
many close together and they'll break each other's
branches. But men like us, the ones who are good enough,
we spring up all over in thick clumps. So we must learn
how to muddle through, how not to rub against each other,
because no one of us has the earth to himself.

TEMPLAR. Fine words. But which nation was the first to set
itself apart? To say 'We are the Chosen People'. Well,
Nathan? This may not be grounds for hatred, I admit, but
can't I still condemn you for your pride? The pride with
which you have infected Christian and Muslim alike, to say
My God Alone Is Right.

You're shocked to hear me talk like this? A Christian, a
Templar and in Jerusalem too. But this mania of claiming
our God's the best and then stamping His claim upon our
brothers, where and when has this been seen more
catastrophically than here and now within Yeru-shalom,
the City of Peace? But the blind are in love with their

blindness and please forget every word I've said and leave me alone

NATHAN. No. Now I will cling to you and never let you leave. We will, we must be friends. Despise my nation all you like. We neither of us chose our people. Must Jews and Christians be always Jews and Christians and only humans afterwards? Or like me will you stand here and say it is enough to be a man?

TEMPLAR. I will, Nathan. I do.

TEMPLAR *offers his hand*. NATHAN *takes it*.

TEMPLAR. Forgive me for misjudging you

NATHAN. I'm proud you did: it's only the commonplace we never misjudge

TEMPLAR. and common you are not. We must, we will be friends

NATHAN. and so we are. And we'll make Rachel very, very happy. Who'll say how this will end? But you must meet her first – and get to know to her.

TEMPLAR. I'm impatient

Enter DAYA.

DAYA. Nathan

NATHAN. yes?

DAYA (*to* TEMPLAR). Excuse me, sir

TEMPLAR. please

NATHAN. What's wrong?

DAYA. The Sultan. Saladin. He's asked to see you.

NATHAN. Are you sure?

DAYA. Sweet Jesus yes the Sultan.

NATHAN. He'll want to see the merchandise I bought in Babylon, he's curious. But I've not unpacked

DAYA. He doesn't want to look at anything. He wants to speak to you, as soon as possible.

NATHAN. I'll come. Go in, I'll come.

DAYA (*to* TEMPLAR). You must forgive us, sir. Dear God, what can he want?

NATHAN. We'll find out soon enough.

DAYA *goes*.

TEMPLAR. Do you know him? The Sultan

NATHAN. not in person. I've not avoided him – but then I haven't sought an audience. Some people say good things, I've no cause to doubt them, and look, he pardoned you so he can't be all bad

TEMPLAR. it's true, I'm his debtor for my life

NATHAN. and so I'm doubly, triply in his debt

TEMPLAR. but I'm still his prisoner and await his final sentence

NATHAN. Well, perhaps I'll have a chance to speak on your behalf. I should go. You'll come to visit us – and soon

TEMPLAR. as is convenient

NATHAN. you decide

TEMPLAR. today

NATHAN. is good. And I suppose that I should ask your name

TEMPLAR. My name was, is Conrad von Stauffen.

NATHAN. von Stauffen?

TEMPLAR. Yes. Is something wrong?

NATHAN. No. I'm sure there must be many von Stauffens

TEMPLAR. There are and many came East and many now rot here. My uncle lies in Gaza, I mean my father –

Why do you stare at me?

NATHAN. Sorry. It's nothing. My friend, I think I'll never tire
of looking at you

TEMPLAR. then I'll leave you, Nathan. Stare too long, you
might see more than you desire. And that I would regret.
Let time confirm our friendship.

Goes.

NATHAN. 'Stare too long, you might see more than you
desire'. You must have read my mind, young Stauffen. But
how could this be? And yet he looks the same. The walk,
the voice, the way that Wolf would hold his head, would
shield his eyes. As if Wolf stood before me – conjured by a
name. Von Stauffen. What angels or demons are working
here? I need to learn more. But first the Sultan.

Enter DAYA.

DAYA. Well, what did he say?

NATHAN. Tell Rachel to expect him at any moment

DAYA. really

NATHAN. really, yes. But Daya, let me handle this in my own
way. Is that clear?

Enter AL-HAFI.

DAYA. Alright – and look, the Sultan's sent for you again.

Goes.

NATHAN. Al-Hafi. He didn't need to send you as well.

AL-HAFI. Who?

NATHAN. Saladin. I've said already I'm coming

AL-HAFI. to the Palace?

NATHAN. Yes. He didn't send you

AL-HAFI. no. But if he's summoned you already

NATHAN. five minutes, not that

AL-HAFI. then it's done

NATHAN. what is? What's done?

AL-HAFI. It's not my fault. God knows it's not my fault.
Nathan, if you'd heard the lies I told them about you. I tried
to lead them off the scent. I did

NATHAN. Hafi, will you stop this gibberish

AL-HAFI. He's got you then

NATHAN. what do you mean

AL-HAFI. you're going to lend him the money

NATHAN. so that's what this is all about.

AL-HAFI. I know you, Nathan, you imagine if you give him
money he'll welcome your advice. But when's Saladin
sought anyone's opinion? Tell me when. Consider what he
did just now, to me:

NATHAN. what's that?

AL-HAFI. His sister had just beaten him at chess when I
arrived, or so he said – they play for money and she's not
too bad. The endgame's still on the board, so you know me
I have to look. Well, he hadn't lost at all

NATHAN. well spotted

AL-HAFI. only had to move his King behind a pawn, he'd be
out of check – I'd show you if we had a set

NATHAN. I'll take your word for it

AL-HAFI. which frees his rook, and then it's mate in three.
I tried to tell him, but

NATHAN. he didn't share your view

AL-HAFI. wouldn't even listen. Throws the board down in a
fit

NATHAN. he does

AL-HAFI. and says it's his choice if he wants to be in mate or
not. I mean, what kind of way is that to play

NATHAN. it's not the way we play, that's for sure

AL-HAFI. and the stake's not nothing. A thousand dinars

NATHAN. but what's that compared to the crime of disregarding the dervish, and on an issue of such incalculable weight? That cries out for vengeance

AL-HAFI. alright, alright. I wanted to warn you about the kind of man you're going to meet, that's all. But I forgot even King Solomon in all his glory was not so wise as you. Trust him if you want to, I wouldn't. And Sittah even less. He may look like an old lion, but his teeth are sharp. I wish you well, and if he asks, you haven't seen me.

Goes.

NATHAN. Well, Nathan, into the lion's den you go. And may the god of Daniel be with you.

Five

A Room in Nathan's House.

RACHEL *and* DAYA.

RACHEL. Daya, were those my father's actual words? Expect him at any moment? That has to mean – I mean it must – he'd be here very soon, if not at once. But all these moments have gone by and where is he?

DAYA. Nathan would have brought him in himself if the damned Sultan hadn't summoned him

RACHEL. I must not cling to what's past. I'll live for all the moments still to come – one of them must bring him to me. But when it does? When my most heartfelt wish has been fulfilled – what then?

DAYA. I'll hope for the fulfilment of my own

RACHEL. what's that?

DAYA. To see you settled as a European bride

RACHEL. You're wrong. I don't want that. Europe may be your home, this is mine.

DAYA. Say what you like, but heaven has its ways. Suppose his God, the God your Templar's fighting for, intends through him to lead you to the land that you were born for?

RACHEL. What are you saying? Sometimes I wonder what gets into you. *His* God? Who can own God? The God he's fighting for? And what sort of God is it that needs people to fight for Him? Not to mention how can I or anyone else be sure what patch of earth we're born for if it's not the one that we were born on. Keep your superstitions to yourself. You've embarrassed me enough with all that angel nonsense. I can't look father in the eye

DAYA. oh yes you won't find reason anywhere but under this roof – well I could tell a tale or two

RACHEL. go on then

A knock at the door.

DAYA. The door

RACHEL. It must be him.

DAYA. Come in.

Enter TEMPLAR.

TEMPLAR. Excuse me, but your father said

DAYA. come in, come in. We've been expecting

This is Rachel

RACHEL *kneels down at his feet.*

TEMPLAR. No. Please. The reason that I haven't been before was to avoid precisely this. You must not

RACHEL. Kneeling before the man who rescued me I give my thanks to God – and not the man. I didn't thank the bucket which so ably let itself be filled and emptied, never giving me the slightest thought, so why him? He just found himself diving into the fire where quite by accident I dropped into his arms, and happened to stick there, like a bit of ash or cinder would until some thing or other swept us both to safety. No point in thanking him for that. In Swabia a beer will inspire a man to more heroic deeds. And anyhow those Templars do all that in basic training, like the better class of hound gets taught to fetch from fire as well as water.

TEMPLAR. Daya, if there were times when through grief or bitterness I lost my temper did you have to relay every stupid word I said?

DAYA. I don't think there's lasting damage.

RACHEL. Tell me about this grief that dogs you. Why do you hug it closer than your life?

TEMPLAR. I wish I could.

But are you sure you're the girl I rescued from the fire?

RACHEL. Why, have I changed?

TEMPLAR. No, I mean wonder why there weren't a hundred men all diving in – the boys that you grew up with, all the Jewish boys, where were they? Who could know you and not try to save you? Why did they wait for me?

I think that fear distorts things, yes?

Pause.

RACHEL. To me you look the same as you did then.

TEMPLAR. I do? I do. That's good.

Pause.

RACHEL. So tell me where you went these last few days?

Silence.

RACHEL. Or maybe I should ask where you are now.

TEMPLAR. I think I'm where perhaps I shouldn't be.

RACHEL. What do you mean?

TEMPLAR. I mean that he was right, Rachel, that once I got to know you

RACHEL. what? Who said that?

TEMPLAR. Nathan. I should find him

RACHEL. why? He's at the Palace

TEMPLAR. still? He can't be. No, I said I'd meet him by the cloister. Idiot. He must be waiting for me. I better go and find him

DAYA. Wait. I'll go. And you can stay with Rachel

TEMPLAR. No, he'll be expecting me. Besides we don't know what has happened at the Palace. It could be dangerous

RACHEL. for who

TEMPLAR. for me, for you, for him. I need to go myself. Forgive me.

Goes.

RACHEL. Daya, what's wrong? What did I do to make him run away?

DAYA. Have no worries. That's a good sign

RACHEL. it is?

DAYA. Something's going on inside. Something's simmering which can't come to the boil. But give him time. And how do you feel now your wish has been fulfilled?

RACHEL. I don't know. Calm. Calmer. I mean I know that I will always love him, that he's dearer to me than my life, but my pulse no longer races at the mention of his name, my heart's stopped pounding at the thought of him.

Come on, I'm going back up to the roof. I just want to look at the palm trees.

Six

An Audience Room in the Sultan's Palace.

SITTAH *and* SALADIN.

SALADIN. Your Jew seems in no hurry to get here.

SITTAH. Maybe he's out. They couldn't find him. Don't be hasty. If we play this rashly it won't work. Nathan's reputation rests upon his wisdom, that's the trap. All you need to do is ask the question calmly. Whatever way he answers he can't win. If he says 'Jew' then he insults you, 'Muslim' why is he a Jew? I think we can assume he won't say Christian

SALADIN. Sister, I

SITTAH. It's not a duel

SALADIN. It is, with weapons I don't understand. Guile and subterfuge. And all to scare some Jew into surrendering his gold

SITTAH. If you don't want to do it, I will

SALADIN. No, I should meet him. But what if he's a decent man? I thought you said he was Al-Hafi's friend

SITTAH. if so, we have no worries. We trap the skulking, stingy Jew, the wise man's ours already. And think of the satisfaction you'll get from watching a truly nimble mind at work. You love all that philosophy, the cutting wit, the painstaking unpicking of an argument

SALADIN. you're right, I do. So by the Prophet may he be the man they say, for all our sakes. You better leave me now, I need some time to think.

SITTAH. But I was going

SALADIN. to stay?

SITTAH. If not here, then in the room next door

SALADIN. and spy on me? No, if I'm doing this, I do it on my own. Without your help. I can hear the outer doors. You better go. Trust me.

As SITTAH *goes through one door,* NATHAN *comes through another.* SALADIN *sits.*

SALADIN. My friend the Jew, come in. Don't look so wary, I don't bite

NATHAN. except your enemies.

SALADIN. Nathan?

NATHAN. Yes

SALADIN. Nathan the Wise?

NATHAN. No.

SALADIN. Of course it's not a name you'd give yourself, but people do

NATHAN. some people, maybe

SALADIN. and you think we should ignore the people's voice? It's long been my ambition to receive the man they call 'The Wise'.

NATHAN. And what if it's a joke at his expense? By 'wise' they mean he always has an eye to his own interest.

SALADIN. But if he understands what truly serves his interest isn't that a kind of wisdom?

NATHAN. If wisdom's only selfishness in robes, then yes.

SALADIN. Come, let's leave false modesty behind, and get to business. You have travelled widely

NATHAN. Sultan, I am at your service. Whatever you require, we'll endeavour to supply it. Our prices aren't the cheapest but the quality's unbeatable

SALADIN. No, no. My sister handles all that. I never deal with tradesmen. What I want to know, is from your travels what you've learnt

NATHAN. of enemy manoeuvres? Well, if I can speak in confidence

SALADIN. No, I've spies enough. That isn't why I asked you here. Nathan

NATHAN. here I stand. Command me

SALADIN. I seek your instruction. You are wise, you've
   travelled, seen the world. Now tell me this: which code,
   which law, which faith have you found most enlightening?

NATHAN. Sultan, I'm a Jew.

SALADIN. And I'm a Muslim. Between us there is
   Christendom. Of these three only one can be the true
   religion.

   A man who thinks about the world like you, doesn't stay
   where accident of birth has cast him. He looks around,
   considers all the options, and if he then comes home, he
   does it with the knowledge that it's best. So share your
   insight with me, Nathan, let me hear the proofs I've not had
   time or wit to fashion for myself. Tell me, in the strictest
   confidence, the choice they've led you to, the real choice,
   and I will make that choice my own. You're shocked. Or
   simply wondering why I've asked the question? I'm not the
   first ruler ever to have sought the truth, it seems to me the
   kind of thing a ruler ought to know. So tell me. Speak. Or
   would you like a moment to collect your thoughts. Take it.
   Think it over.

   Goes out the way SITTAH *went.*

NATHAN. I came prepared to give him money – what he
   wants is truth. The truth. And wants it handed out like
   money. Like something you can jingle in your purse. Maybe
   it is. Maybe the truth is just a coin whose value's weighed
   and stamped upon it underneath the portrait of a king.

   And why do I assume he's not sincere? Because he is a
   Muslim, I'm a Jew? Because his armies occupy my land?
   Prejudice, or common sense?

   So what's your answer, Nathan? Play the orthodox and risk
   his wrath? Deny your race and chance the question then
   'why aren't you a Muslim?' These won't work. It needs
   another path. It needs another kind of answer. Is that it? Is
   that the way? A child's fable to bewitch a Sultan.

   Enter SALADIN.

SALADIN. Am I back too soon? D'you need more time?

NATHAN. No, I'm ready

SALADIN. so speak. There's not a soul to hear us

NATHAN. I'd be happy if the whole world could hear us

SALADIN. that's what I call wisdom. The wise man never hides the truth. He'll shout it from the rooftops. He'll stake his life upon it

NATHAN. if he must. But first, I'd like to share a little story if there's time

SALADIN. there's always time to hear a story, if the story-teller's good

NATHAN. that I can't guarantee

SALADIN. false modesty again. Come on, begin:

NATHAN. Once in the East there lived a man who owned a ring of unimaginable worth. It bore a jewel in which a thousand colours played and had the power to make the wearer loved by all people, and by God. No wonder that this man would never let it leave his finger or that he resolved that it should never leave his family. He bequeathed it to his favourite son and with it the instruction he in turn should pass it to his favourite son and that henceforth, ignoring all priority of birth, the favourite son should be the master of the house by virtue of the power of the ring. Do you follow

SALADIN. yes. Go on:

NATHAN. From favourite son to favourite son the ring passed down the ages till it came to a father who had three sons. All equally obedient, all equally attentive, all equally loved by their father. And so, according to which son pleased him most, at the end of a long day spent riding or talking, the embers dying in the grate, one by one he pledges the ring to each. Death approaches, and now the father is dismayed. He cannot bear to think that two of his sons have trusted him and now must be denied. So he sends in secret for a jeweller and commissions him to make two copies, sparing neither cost nor effort till they are identical with the true ring. The

jeweller obeys and when the rings are brought even the
father can't tell which is the original and which the fakes.
Joyfully he summons his sons one by one and gives to each
his blessing and his ring. And so he dies.

Are you with me still

SALADIN. I am. And want to know the end. What happened?

NATHAN. That's it. I've reached the end. What happened
next's predictable. The father's scarcely breathed his last
before each brother comes with his ring and claims to be
the master of the house. They haggle, they argue, they fight.
In vain. No one can prove which is the true ring.

Pause.

Just as today no one can prove which is the true faith.

SALADIN. And that's your answer to my question

NATHAN. No, it's my excuse. For not being able to
distinguish between three rings which the father had
contrived to be indistinguishable.

SALADIN. I'm not a child, Jew. The three religions which I
named to you are quite distinct. In liturgy, in dress, in food

NATHAN. superficially, of course. But all three have equally
their roots in history. In memory. In things that were written
or handed down. Such things as must be taken on trust.
Faith. And whose faith do we trust most? Our own of
course. The faith that we were raised in, the faith that runs
in our blood, and in the blood of those who loved us since
we were children. And who have never deceived us, unless
for our own good. How should I trust my ancestors less
than you yours? Or vice versa. How can I demand that you
denounce yours simply so that mine are vindicated? Or vice
versa.

SALADIN. Agreed

NATHAN. but still you want an answer.

Let me return to our rings. As I said, the sons argued. They
brought the case before a judge. Each made a statement,

swearing that he'd received his ring directly from the
father's hand. Which was true. That the father had promised
him the ring at the end of a long day spent riding or talking,
when the embers were dying etc. Which was also true. And
each declared the father couldn't possibly have deceived
him and that – much as he loved his brothers – it must be
one of them to blame, and he would soon expose the traitor
and then take his revenge.

SALADIN. And what did the judge say? That's what we want
to know

NATHAN. The judge said this: 'This case will only be resolved
if you can bring your father to the witness stand. Which you
can't. Or if the true ring makes a statement. Which seems
unlikely. Failing that, I must dismiss the case. But wait, I've
heard the power of this ring is to make the wearer loved by
God and by all people. Maybe that's your clue. The false
rings could not do this. So think, which brother do the
others love the most? Tell me. Or does each brother only
love himself? If so then you're all deceived and all your
rings are false. Perhaps the true one was mislaid, and the
father had these three copies made as a replacement'.

SALADIN. Very good

NATHAN. 'And so,' the judge went on, 'if what you want's a
verdict, you must go elsewhere. But if you'll take advice,
I'll tell you this: Accept the situation as it is. Each of you
has a ring from your father, have faith that it's the true one.
Maybe this was your father's plan, to end the tyranny of the
single ring. It's clear he loved you all, and loved you
equally: why should he disadvantage two by favouring one?
You could do worse than follow his example, strive towards
such unprejudiced affection in yourselves. Vie with each
other to prove the power of your ring, through gentleness,
tolerance, charity, and a deep humility before the love of
God. And if after a thousand thousand years the power of
the ring still shines amongst your children's children's
children, then I'll summon you again before this judgement
seat. A wiser man than I shall then preside and he will give
his verdict.'

SALADIN. God.

NATHAN. These were the words of the modest judge.

SALADIN. God is merciful.

NATHAN. If you believe yourself to be this promised wiser judge

SALADIN. I am dust. I am nothing.

SALADIN *takes* NATHAN*'s hand and holds it for a long time*.

NATHAN. What is it, Sultan?

SALADIN. Nathan, my friend. Your judge's thousand thousand years are not yet past. His judgement seat is not mine. You may go, but forever be my friend.

NATHAN. You've nothing more to ask me?

SALADIN. No.

NATHAN. You're sure?

SALADIN. Nothing at all. Why d'you ask?

NATHAN. I'd hoped to beg a favour

SALADIN. no need to beg:

NATHAN. As you may know, I returned from Babylon today, collecting debts as I came. And now I've all this money in the house. The times grow more uncertain and I don't know what to do with it. I was thinking – war's an expensive business – maybe you could put it to good use

SALADIN. Has Al-Hafi been to see you? No, I won't ask. I accept your offer in the spirit that it's given.

NATHAN. I'd lend you all of it, but I've promised something to the young Templar

SALADIN. A Templar? Are you funding my enemies as well?

NATHAN. I meant the man whose life you spared

SALADIN. him? How do you know him?

NATHAN. You haven't heard how I benefited from your compassion? Hardly had you spared his life than he was risking it to save my daughter from a fire

SALADIN. he was? He looked the kind who might. My brother Assad would have done the same. They are alike in many ways.

So where's he now, this Templar? Can you bring him here? My sister never knew our brother, but I've talked so much about him I at least should let her meet his twin. Please, fetch him. He saved your daughter, did he? From one good deed how many others flow.

NATHAN. I'll find him. And the rest is as we agreed?

Goes.

SALADIN. I should have let Sittah stay. How on earth am I going to tell her all this?

Seven

The palm-grove. The TEMPLAR *pacing. Stops.*

TEMPLAR. Here the dead man rests his bones.

I've had enough of trying to make sense of how I feel. I daren't imagine what will come. I ran away. I ran away.

But what else could I do? To see the girl I never wished to see again, and in a flash to feel bound to her, woven in her being. To live apart from her is death. And in whatever place we go to after death, there still death.

So I'm in love. A Templar is in love. A Christian loves a Jew. What d'you expect? This is the Promised Land. And I have lost a legion of prejudice.

As Templar I am dead. The Order's grip is loosed. But I was dead already from the moment I was captured. And the life that Saladin returned was not my own. It is another man

who leaves the scaffold, and his life is free of all that I'd
been taught, of all I'd lived. A man more like my father.

For I stand under the same sky, on the same earth where he
once stood, and all the stories of him are alive. It must be
true. For I've fallen where he fell.

What more incitement do I need to love Rachel? Nathan's
approval. That won't be hard to win.

Enter NATHAN.

TEMPLAR. Nathan. You look happy. Then doesn't everyone
when leaving Saladin.

NATHAN. You're here. Good. He wants to see you as soon as
possible. We'll go together. But there's something I need to
do for him at home first, so come in and then

TEMPLAR. I can't

NATHAN. I'll only be a moment

TEMPLAR. I can't enter your house again.

NATHAN. You've been in already? You've seen Rachel?
Well? How did it go? Did you like her?

TEMPLAR. Beyond all words. But I can never look at her
again

NATHAN. why not

TEMPLAR. unless you promise me this instant I shall gaze
upon her always.

NATHAN. Ah. I see.

Pause.

TEMPLAR *suddenly throws himself around NATHAN's
neck.*

TEMPLAR. Father

NATHAN. please. Young man

TEMPLAR. Not son? Nathan

NATHAN. my dear young man

TEMPLAR. Say son. Please. I beg you. Nathan. 'Must Jews
and Christians be firstly Jews and Christians and only
humans after?' 'Won't you say that it's enough to be a
man?' Don't turn me away.

NATHAN. My dear friend

TEMPLAR. say son. Why not son?

NATHAN. You've surprised me. I need to think

TEMPLAR. Nathan, it was your idea. Don't you remember?
You wanted us to get to know each other. How can you be
surprised?

NATHAN. I need to ask you something. There is something I
need to know. You said your father's name was von
Stauffen

TEMPLAR. yes. But what's my father matter? Judge me for
myself

NATHAN. you see – I've met a Stauffen once before, whose
name was also Conrad

TEMPLAR. so? And what if that's my father's name

NATHAN. was it? You must tell me:

TEMPLAR. I was named after my father. Conrad von Stauffen

NATHAN. then these are different men. My Conrad was like
you a Templar and so never married

TEMPLAR. That need not have prevented him from being my
father

NATHAN. you're joking with me

TEMPLAR. and you are quick to disapprove. But if you'll
inquire no further into my pedigree, then I won't inquire into
yours. Not that I'm suggesting anything's wrong with it. God
forbid. I bet your family tree has every leaf accounted for all
the way back to Abraham. And before probably.

NATHAN. What have I done to provoke this? Why are you so
angry with me? I need time that's all. I need certain
information – which you have given me. Now please come

in. We'll talk some more about this later. The Sultan's
waiting.

TEMPLAR. No, I can't. Not until you give your word. There
is a fire in there.

NATHAN. As you wish. Wait here.

Goes.

TEMPLAR. If I see her again, then I must see her forever. If
not, then I've already gazed too long.

Enter DAYA.

DAYA. Sir

TEMPLAR. Who's that?

DAYA. Come over here. He'll see us where you are.

TEMPLAR. Daya? What's the matter? Why the secrecy?

DAYA. I have a secret, yes. And so do you. You tell me yours
and then I'll tell you mine

TEMPLAR. gladly. But I don't know what you think my secret
is. So you'll have to tell me yours first:

DAYA. No, that won't work. My secret's no use to you until
you've told me yours

TEMPLAR. right. So what do we do? I'm not in the mood for
games.

DAYA. Very well, tell me this: why did you vanish so
suddenly? With no explanation. Left us sitting there. And
why wouldn't you come in with Nathan now? Is it because
Rachel doesn't appeal to you – or because she appeals too
much?

Please tell me that's it. Tell me that you love her to
distraction and then I'll

TEMPLAR. distraction? To madness itself

DAYA. Yes! Tell me about it. The love, the madness I can
imagine

TEMPLAR. because it's obviously mad a Templar loving a
Jew

DAYA. shouldn't happen, should it? Welcome to the land of
miracles

TEMPLAR. and what else could it be, when all the peoples of
the earth are crammed together here. Yes, Daya, if that's the
secret that you wanted to hear: I love her. And I have no
idea how to live without her. So, what do you have to tell
me?

DAYA. No, first you must swear to me that you'll marry her:

TEMPLAR. I can't

DAYA. you must. Swear that and you will save her once again,
not only in this life, but for all eternity:

TEMPLAR. I can't swear that because it's not in my power

DAYA. it is

TEMPLAR. why? Has Nathan changed his mind?

DAYA. I don't understand. You've already approached him?

TEMPLAR. Just now

DAYA. what happened?

TEMPLAR. I lost my temper

DAYA. with him? why? How?

TEMPLAR. Let's say we weren't singing from the same sheet.

DAYA. Are you telling me you showed even the slightest
interest in Rachel and he didn't jump for joy?

TEMPLAR. He insulted me.

DAYA. Then you will have to know. I can keep silent no
longer.

Rachel is not a Jew. She was born a Christian, to Christian
parents, baptised by them

TEMPLAR. and Nathan is

DAYA. not her father.

TEMPLAR. Are you certain?

DAYA. It's a truth that's cost me tears of blood. Nathan is not her father.

TEMPLAR. But he raised her as his daughter? He raised a Christian child as a Jew?

DAYA. Yes.

TEMPLAR. Does she know this?

DAYA. No.

TEMPLAR. She's not been told?

DAYA. Never.

TEMPLAR. But she's a grown woman.

DAYA. He's never told her anything.

TEMPLAR. Nathan, how? How could you do it? How could you be guilty of such perversion?

Daya, this – something must be done, I don't know what, I don't know what I should do. I need time to think. You better go – he'll be out again soon and he shouldn't see us together. Go.

DAYA. He would kill me, if he knew

TEMPLAR. I can't possibly speak to him now. If you see him, say that I'll make my own way to the Palace and find him there.

DAYA. But he mustn't see that you know anything. That could be all the excuse that he needs to

TEMPLAR. to what?

DAYA. While Rachel is still in his charge, we have to be careful, that's all. But if you decide to take her to Europe with you, promise you won't leave me behind?

TEMPLAR. We'll see. Now go. Quickly.

Eight

The cloisters of the monastery.

*The Lay-*BROTHER *alone.*

BROTHER. The Patriarch is never wrong. So why do I fail at every task he gives me? To be honest, I wish he'd ask somebody else. I can't be subtle and persuasive. I'm no good at sticking my nose into other people's business. It isn't why I left the world behind.

Enter TEMPLAR.

TEMPLAR. Good brother, I've been looking for you

BROTHER. for me?

TEMPLAR. You remember who I am

BROTHER. yes, but I didn't expect to see you again. To be honest I rather hoped I wouldn't

TEMPLAR. What do you mean?

BROTHER. Only that I was a little embarrassed by our earlier meeting. But I take it you've reconsidered

TEMPLAR. No, that's not why I'm here. I haven't changed my mind about that. I need to consult the Patriarch.

BROTHER. What does a soldier want with a priest's advice?

TEMPLAR. Because there are some things I'd rather do badly by another's counsel, than well by my own. And if I've learnt nothing else here, it's that religion's about party politics and if you try to be a lone wolf, all the packs will unite against you. So I need to know that I have somebody's right on my side.

BROTHER. I think I better find the Patriarch

TEMPLAR. No, wait. Maybe I don't need to see him. Maybe you can be my Patriarch. The situation is this

BROTHER. Please, sir. You have the wrong man. He who knows many things, has many cares. But we're in luck, here comes the Patriarch himself

TEMPLAR. those robes would put Saladin to shame

BROTHER. oh no, you should see him on his way to court. Today he's just been visiting the sick.

Enter the PATRIARCH.

BROTHER. Father, this is

PATRIARCH. the brave young Templar. Introductions are superfluous. And young is the operative word. Yes, with God's help, you'll come to something, my son

TEMPLAR. not much more than I have already, I fear, your Eminence

PATRIARCH. at the least I hope your courage and piety will continue to bring glory to both Our Lord and His Church. Our seasoned heads need youthful valour. And vice versa. You may leave us, Brother Bonafides. But don't go far.

BROTHER *falls back*.

PATRIARCH. How can I assist you?

TEMPLAR. By providing what my youth lacks: guidance

PATRIARCH. always happy to. Though remember that guidance is not given casually. Those who give it expect it to be followed.

TEMPLAR. Not followed blindly?

PATRIARCH. To whom have you been talking? No. Our Father gave us reason and free will, and we must use them whenever and wherever appropriate.

TEMPLAR. When would they be inappropriate?

PATRIARCH. Is this the matter on which you've come to consult me?

TEMPLAR. It might be:

PATRIARCH. Then let us say that God revealed to us a course of action through which the Christian mission of Grace and Charity might be advanced on earth, although in a manner which might seem peculiar, even barbaric – should we then place reason in the path of Him who created reason? Or should we act with faith, acknowledging how much greater is His wisdom than our own.

TEMPLAR. Suppose then, reverend father, that a Jew has an only child, for the sake of argument, a daughter. He has raised her with the utmost care for her moral education. He loves her more than his soul and she has always returned his love.

PATRIARCH. You are saying that albeit that he is a Jew, he has been a good father

TEMPLAR. the best. But supposing it came to our attention that the girl was not his daughter, that he had found her, bought her, maybe stolen her as a baby, I don't know; that she was a Christian child, baptised.

PATRIARCH. The Jew has raised her as a Jew?

TEMPLAR. Solely as a Jew. She has no idea that she is anything but Jewish and his daughter. What should be done?

PATRIARCH. First, you must clarify something for me. Is this an actual case or merely a hypothesis?

TEMPLAR. I don't see how that would affect your opinion

PATRIARCH. because if this appalling scenario is merely a piece of intellectual caprice, it is not worthy of serious consideration. And I'd suggest you went out and found the nearest theatre where you'll find such speculations regularly bandied back and forth for the audience's edification and delight. But if you have come in good faith, and you wish to tell me that this affair has taken place, is taking place within this diocese, within the walls of the Holy City

TEMPLAR. then

PATRIARCH. action must be taken in accord with papal and imperial law

TEMPLAR. so

PATRIARCH. the penalty of both codes is explicit. A Jew found guilty of leading a Christian into apostasy must be burnt at the stake

Well?

And think how much worse it is when it's a child who has
been ripped from the cradle of baptism. Every act done to a
child is an act of violence unless it is sanctioned by the
Church herself.

TEMPLAR. But what if the child would have died in misery
if the Jew hadn't saved her?

PATRIARCH. It is better to die in misery on earth, than to be
preserved for eternal damnation. The Jew must burn. And
who is he to pre-empt the Will of God, who can save
whomever He wishes without the assistance of a Jew

TEMPLAR. and perhaps also in spite of it

PATRIARCH. The Jew must burn.

TEMPLAR. But suppose that he hasn't raised her in his faith,
but in no faith at all. That he's taught her only what she
needs to know of God to satisfy her intellectual inquiry

PATRIARCH. For this alone he would deserve burning three
times over. How should a child grow up without faith? How
should a child be left utterly ignorant of our greatest duty?
To believe. The thought makes my flesh crawl. I'm
astonished that as a Templar, as a Christian, as a man you
can contemplate this so calmly

TEMPLAR. Your Eminence, thank you for your advice and
I shall bear it in mind but now

Starts to go.

PATRIARCH. You can't leave the matter there. If this is fact,
then you must name this Jew. It is your duty as a Knight of
Christ to bring him before us. What is his name?

TEMPLAR. No more, your Eminence, outside the
confessional.

PATRIARCH. Very well. But there are other ways of finding
him. Under the terms of the city's surrender the Sultan is
bound to protect us, and to defend the laws and the
doctrines of our faith. We have a copy of the capitulation

here in the monastery which bears his signature and his
seal. I know Saladin well enough to know that he will
swiftly understand the threat that atheism poses to civil
order. Once people have no belief in God, why should they
hold any other bonds sacred? They will tear the state
asunder. I think he will be ready to see this abomination
expunged from the city.

TEMPLAR. I'm sorry that I can't stay to appreciate your
inspirational words, but I'm invited to the Palace myself

PATRIARCH. you are

TEMPLAR. so if you like I can alert Saladin to your coming

PATRIARCH. I've heard you count him among your friends

TEMPLAR. yes, Brother Bonafides made it very clear how
you thought I should repay that friendship.

PATRIARCH. Well, perhaps you'd send the Sultan my regards.
He of all men understands how when one is driven by zeal
for God's truth, one can sometimes over-step the mark. And
what you were saying about the Jew, that was just
conjecture

TEMPLAR. conjecture, yes

Goes.

PATRIARCH. whose basis I must examine further. Another
task for Brother Bonafides, I think.

(*To* BROTHER.) Join me.

PATRIARCH *leaves in conversation with the* BROTHER.

Nine

A Room in the Palace.

SITTAH *with a picture. Enter* SALADIN.

SALADIN. Where's Al-Hafi? The Templar's here and Nathan
will be bringing his gold. What's that?

SITTAH. I found it.

SALADIN. It's him. It's Assad. My brave brother. What we
two might have achieved. Where did you find this?

SITTAH. In a box.

SALADIN. I remember it. He gave it to your older sister, to
his Lilla, one morning when she absolutely would not let
him leave the house. She clung to him. It was the last time
he rode out. And I let him go alone. Lilla never forgave me.
He did not return.

SITTAH. Poor brother

SALADIN. God's will be done. One day we shall all ride out
and not return. But we should use this to compare him with
the Templar. See if my memory is playing tricks.

SITTAH. That's why I brought it. But give it to me. Women
are much better at comparing men.

SITTAH *throws herself onto a sofa to one side and drops
her veil.*

Don't worry, I won't disturb you. And I'll try not to let my
curiosity disturb him.

Enter TEMPLAR.

TEMPLAR. Your prisoner, Sultan

SALADIN. My prisoner? Do you think I won't add freedom to
the life I've granted you already?

TEMPLAR. I regret Sultan that saying thank you isn't easy
for me, that is I don't do it well. And I don't know how
I should begin to thank you for my life, except to say that
it is always at your service.

SALADIN. All I ask is that it's not put in the service of my
enemies. I don't begrudge them the extra pair of hands, but
I can't spare them your spirit.

I feared seeing you again, I feared the disappointment. But
you have not disappointed me. Body and soul you are my
brother Assad. I want to remind you of past exploits, fight
with you over all the secrets you've kept from me – how
could you go off on an adventure without me? And I'd do
it, if I could see only you and not myself as well – for you
are as he was and I, well at least this much of my dream is
truth: in the autumn of my years a new Assad has
blossomed.

Stay with me. Stay here beside me. As Christian or Muslim,
you decide, in tunic, djellaba, helmet, turban, it doesn't
matter. In my garden the trees bear many different kinds of
fruit.

TEMPLAR. Then you are as the world says a hero who longs
to be God's Gardener.

SALADIN. And if you think none the worse of me for that,
then we must be half-agreed.

TEMPLAR. No. We are agreed.

SALADIN (*holding out his hand*). Your hand

TEMPLAR (*taking it*). your man. And receive more than you
could ever have taken from me.

SALADIN. This is too much for one day.

So, where's our friend? Didn't he come with you?

TEMPLAR. Who?

SALADIN. Who else? Nathan.

TEMPLAR. No, I came alone.

SALADIN. That's a pity.

But what a service you did for him. You couldn't have
helped a better man.

TEMPLAR. So they say.

SALADIN. My young friend, when God chooses to do good through us, we should not appear indifferent to it, even out of modesty.

TEMPLAR. But everything has so many different faces, and sometimes I don't understand how they can all belong together

SALADIN. Then you should seek the best in everything, and trust God who knows how all things are connected.

TEMPLAR. Maybe.

SALADIN. Young man, if you're going to be so hard to please, we'll have to watch each other. I too am a thing of many faces, which may also appear to you irreconcilable.

TEMPLAR. I'm very rarely suspicious of people

SALADIN. so why now? And why as it seems of Nathan?

If we are to be friends, then you must tell me.

TEMPLAR. I've nothing against Nathan. Nathan is Nathan. I'm angry with myself

SALADIN. why?

TEMPLAR. For dreaming that a Jew could cease to be Jew. For dreaming it with my eyes wide open.

SALADIN. Tell me:

TEMPLAR. Nathan's daughter. I did for her what I did because I did it. But I didn't want her thanks, I didn't want anything from them, so I refused to see her, despite many requests. Nathan comes home, he learns what's happened, he seeks me out, he thanks me, we

he hopes that I might grow to like his daughter. So having been persuaded I come to the house, and there I find a girl, a girl of

I am ashamed of myself

SALADIN. why? For being attracted to a Jew? Is that all?

TEMPLAR. If Nathan hadn't encouraged me, then maybe
I could have resisted but I am a fool. I leapt into the flames
again. And this time I was rejected

SALADIN. by who? The girl?

TEMPLAR. Nathan. Oh, he doesn't dismiss me outright. No,
he's too shrewd for that. He has to make enquiries, think
things over, needs time. Well, we could all do that. Why
didn't I take some time to consider the situation while the
flames were licking at her ankles? That would have been
wise.

SALADIN. He's an old man. You must make allowance for us.
If he needs time then that's what he needs. It's not as if he's
asking you to convert

TEMPLAR. who knows

SALADIN. those who know Nathan better than you.

TEMPLAR. You think he has no prejudices just because he
appears so rational, so open-minded? I don't believe we
ever lose the superstitions of our race. We drink them in
with our mother's milk, and we may mock them but they
are bred into our bones

SALADIN. you may be right in general, but we are talking
about Nathan

TEMPLAR. and sometimes they are so ingrained we don't
even know they're there, and sometimes we indulge them
because they are our own

SALADIN. yes, but no one could accuse Nathan of this.

TEMPLAR. I thought so too. And what if you heard this
paragon was actually so fervent in his faith that he sought to
obtain Christian children and raise them up as Jews?

SALADIN. Who's told you this?

TEMPLAR. The girl, the same girl he lured me with, the girl
he says is his daughter, is no such thing. She's a Christian
child taken from God knows where

SALADIN. and whom he will not let you have

TEMPLAR. whether he will or won't, does it matter? He's
  unmasked. The prophet of tolerance is shown for what he is.
  A Jewish wolf.

SALADIN. Calm down.

TEMPLAR. Why should I be calm? Why should Jews and
  Muslims have their rights and Christians be denied?

SALADIN. Calm down

TEMPLAR. and now you begin to withdraw from me. I can
  hear it in your voice. You no longer feel the same affection
  for me. Tell me how Assad would have acted in my place.

SALADIN. Not much better. And with the same sound and
  fury. Who's taught you to get round me with a word like
  only he could?

  I'll admit, if what you're saying's true, then Nathan is not
  the man I thought. But he is my friend, and I do not like my
  friends fighting with each other. So take my advice: tread
  carefully. Go and find Nathan and bring him here. I will see
  you both reconciled. Above all say nothing of this to the
  fanatics of your faith. Never be a Christian to spite a Jew.
  Or a Muslim.

  TEMPLAR *goes*.

SITTAH. Remarkable.

SALADIN. Well, will you finally accept that Assad was as
  brave and handsome as I've always said?

SITTAH. If it wasn't the Templar who sat for this picture.

SALADIN. Nathan must give him the girl, don't you agree?

SITTAH. Is she his to give, that's the question

SALADIN. and if not, why shouldn't the rights of the father
  fall to the man who saved her life?

SITTAH. Brother, why don't you bring her to the Palace?
  While the situation's uncertain, take her into your care.

SALADIN. Do you think we need to?

SITTAH. Need? Maybe not. But with some men I long to know what kind of girls they fall for.

SALADIN. Then why not send for her yourself?

SITTAH. Can I do that?

SALADIN. So long as you treat Nathan with respect. He mustn't think we're taking her away from him.

SITTAH. You know me, I'll be discretion itself.

SALADIN. And I shall go and find where Al-Hafi has got to.

Ten

The courtyard of Nathan's House.

NATHAN *with money. To him,* AL-HAFI, *no longer in his robes.*

AL-HAFI. You've got it bagged and ready then

NATHAN. this is the money I'm taking to the Sultan, yes

AL-HAFI. well, I won't stay around to see it. I'm going, right now. You know where. If there's anything you want me to take away for you, let me know. Though it can't be more than a naked beggar can carry. Come on, I'm not waiting

NATHAN. Hafi, will you pull yourself together? What are you doing?

AL-HAFI. Don't think this'll be the end of it. And you expect me to stand by day after day while he bleeds you dry? Do you want me to witness that?

Well, I've had it with him. I've had it with running back and forth trying to find someone who'll lend him something. Me, who's never begged for myself. Borrowing is no better than begging, and usury's the same as theft. Beside the Ganges I won't have need of either. Beside the Ganges a man is just a man.

You are the only one in this whole city worthy of the life
there. Come with me. Let him have the money. Pile the
whole lot up and send it to him. Come with me.

NATHAN. Y'know I always thought that's how you and I
would end up. The two of us beside the Ganges

AL-HAFI. so let's go

NATHAN. I need to think about it. Can't you wait

AL-HAFI. this isn't something you think about

NATHAN. until I get back from the palace, until I've said
goodbye

AL-HAFI. think about it and you'll find a reason not to do it.
If you cannot live your life in the instant, then you will
always be the slave of others. It's your choice.

Pause.

May you be happy in the life that you seek. My path goes
that way, and yours this.

NATHAN. Al-Hafi. You can't leave like that. Don't you need
to settle the accounts?

AL-HAFI. The accounts, don't make me laugh. There's
nothing there apart from debts. And you'll vouch for them.

Be happy.

Goes.

NATHAN. I'll vouch for you you, mad, kind, good – what
shall I say? Maybe you're right: maybe a beggar is the only
true sovereign.

Enter DAYA.

DAYA. There's a friar at the gate

NATHAN. Well, take him this

DAYA. No, he doesn't want money. He wants to speak to you.
He says it won't take long

NATHAN. very well, show him in.

DAYA *lingers*.

NATHAN. What is it, Daya?

DAYA. Don't pretend you don't know. The Templar loves
Rachel. Let him have her. Put an end to your sin, because I
can't keep silent any longer.

NATHAN. A few days, that's all I ask. A few days more. Now
show in the friar. And then leave us.

DAYA *goes. Returns with the* BROTHER *and leaves*.

Holy brother, what can I do for you?

BROTHER. I'm delighted to see the great Nathan looking so
well.

NATHAN. Do you know me?

BROTHER. Who doesn't? You've pressed your name into
enough palms along the years. Mine amongst them

NATHAN. then allow me to refresh it now

BROTHER. thank you, but I'd be stealing from those poorer
than myself. Instead let me refresh my name with you. For I
once placed something precious into your hands.

NATHAN. You did? I must apologise. Tell me what it was and
then you must take seven times its worth in atonement for
my forgetfulness.

BROTHER. First I should apologise for having myself
forgotten about this bond until today

NATHAN. you entrusted a bond with me

BROTHER. Allow me. Some while ago I lived as a hermit not
far from Jericho. One day a gang of Arab youths – it was
the time of reprisals – came by my cell. They smashed up
the shrine, dragged me into the street, I was lucky to escape
with my life. I fled here, to the Patriarch's protection, and to
request another cell where I might serve God in solitude
until He chooses to release me from this world.

NATHAN. Good brother, please enlighten me. What is this
bond you entrusted with me?

BROTHER. I'll come to that, Nathan. But first you should know that the Patriarch promised me a cell upon Mount Tabor as soon as one falls vacant, and in the meantime I must remain in the monastery as a lay-brother. Since then he has taken to employing me in a number of tasks which I find distasteful. For example

NATHAN. To the point, please

BROTHER. We have reached it. Today the Patriarch received information concerning a Jew in this city, who it's alleged has raised a Christian child as his own daughter.

NATHAN. From where has he heard this?

BROTHER. Hear me out. Even as he's instructing me to track the Jew down and winding himself into a fury over this abomination, I feel a sinking in my heart, because it occurs to me that it could be I myself who has given rise to this unpardonable sin.

NATHAN. You? I don't understand.

BROTHER. Look at me, Nathan. Are you sure you don't recognise me?

NATHAN. I could swear I've never seen you before today.

BROTHER. Then tell me, eighteen years ago did a Christian soldier come to your door, carrying a baby girl just a few weeks old?

NATHAN. I – yes

BROTHER. look again

NATHAN. you?

BROTHER. And the knight who sent me, her father, his name I think was Vilnek

NATHAN. yes, it was.

BROTHER. Her mother had died, and he had been posted at short notice to Gaza, as I remember, somewhere where he couldn't possibly have taken the girl, and so he sent her to you, his friend. I found you at Darun, is that right?

NATHAN. I was staying there, yes.

BROTHER. Well, I wouldn't have been surprised if my memory had tricked me. I served so many knights in those days, and this one died soon after at Ascalon. But he was a good man.

NATHAN. He was. I've much to thank him for. He shielded me on more than one occasion.

BROTHER. Then you must have been very happy to be able to take care of his daughter

NATHAN. more than you can imagine.

BROTHER. Who else knows this?

NATHAN. Only the woman who cares for her, and she only in part

BROTHER. then there's still hope

NATHAN. What do you mean? Hope of what?

BROTHER. You must trust me, Nathan, for I rarely meddle in such affairs: I'd sooner stand aside than risk committing a sin by trying to do good. But I don't believe there was anything unnatural in the way you raised the child. You did it with your whole heart and soul and don't deserve to be treated as a devil. I won't stand by and see that. Maybe it would have been more prudent to put her into the care of a Christian family, but this was the child of a friend. When they are small children need love, even the love of a wild animal, more than they need Christianity. So what could be wrong with the love of a Jew? Wasn't our Lord Jesus a Jew?

NATHAN. Brother, if hypocrisy and hatred are stirred up against me, I hope you'll speak on my behalf. I do trust you, and I will tell you what no one has ever heard, and which you must take with you to your grave. Because I trust in your piety you will comprehend what it means to surrender oneself to the Will of God.

BROTHER. Tell me, if you wish.

NATHAN. You met me with the child at Darun. But you were not to know that just a few days earlier in Gath the

Christians had murdered every single Jew. Women and children also. Nor could you know that amongst them were my wife and seven sons, burned alive in my brother's house, where they had taken refuge.

BROTHER. Almighty God

NATHAN. When you appeared, I had spent three days in dust and ashes stretched out before God, weeping – weeping and raging at Him, raving, cursing myself and all His creation. I had sworn unending hatred to all Christians

BROTHER. I can well believe you.

NATHAN. But gradually reason returned to me. I heard a gentle voice saying: 'But still God remains. This too is God's work. So, come. It is time to practise what you have long since understood. It will be no harder to practise than it was to understand, if only you have the will. Get up.'

I stood and cried out to God: I will. If it is Your Will that I should. And at that moment you got down off your horse and presented me with a child bundled up in your coat. What words passed between us, I've forgotten. I only remember taking her, putting her on the bed, kissing her, before I fell down on my knees and sobbed: My God, I have one of the seven again.

BROTHER. Nathan, you are a Christian. By Our Lord a truer Christian never lived.

NATHAN. What makes me a Christian to you, makes you a Jew to me. Enough with tears. There's work to be done. For though a sevenfold love has bound me to this child of a foreign land, and though the thought kills me that in losing her I lose my sons once more – if the God of my salvation demands her of me, I shall obey.

BROTHER. It is the way.

NATHAN. So, my friend, you must tell me of some brother or uncle, some relation, I'll not withhold her from him: she was born and raised to be the glory of any family, and of any faith.

BROTHER. I fear I cannot help. I served him so briefly, and it was long ago.

NATHAN. The mother, then. His wife. Her name was Stauffen

BROTHER. yes, I remember

NATHAN. and her brother was Conrad von Stauffen, and was a Knight Templar

BROTHER. you knew them better than I

NATHAN. But did you keep nothing of your master's? Any pictures, or papers

BROTHER. only a little book. It was in his tunic when we buried him at Ascalon

NATHAN. where is it now?

BROTHER. I brought it for the girl. As her one bequest from her father. Besides yourself.

Hands NATHAN *the book.*

BROTHER. It has prayers in it. We call it a breviary.

NATHAN. It has more than prayers, my friend. Do you see this writing

BROTHER. what does it say? Is it Arabic?

NATHAN. It's a list of names. It is her family.

Enter DAYA.

DAYA. Nathan, you must do something.

NATHAN. What is it?

DAYA. The poor child is scared out of her wits. Someone's come

BROTHER. from the Patriarch?

DAYA. No. From the Sultan's sister

NATHAN. Sittah?

DAYA. She wants to see Rachel.

NATHAN. Not from the Patriarch?

DAYA. Are you deaf? No, the Sultan's sister. Why would the Patriarch be interested in Rachel?

NATHAN. I don't know, Daya. Perhaps you could tell me:

DAYA. What are we going to do?

NATHAN. I can see no harm in Rachel going to the Palace

DAYA. But the only daughter of a rich Jew would be an attractive proposition even to a Muslim, Nathan. We must tell the boy

NATHAN. Daya, there is nothing to worry about. Take Rachel to see the Sultan's sister, and tell her that I shall be at the Palace soon myself – and with joyful news.

DAYA. Are you going to tell her the truth?

NATHAN. In good time, Daya, in good time.

DAYA. End it, Nathan. Because if you don't, I will.

Goes.

BROTHER. You're going to the Palace

NATHAN. yes, and with your permission, brother, I would like to take this little book with me. I will pay you for it, its weight in gold and a thousand dinars more

BROTHER. It's not mine to sell. It belongs to his daughter. I hope God may never cause you to regret all that you've done for her

NATHAN. that could never be. Have no fear

BROTHER. except of Patriarchs and Templars.

NATHAN. Templars? Do you mean it was a Templar who informed the Patriarch?

BROTHER. I fear it must have been. A Templar had just spoken with him when he summoned me, and though I only heard a little

NATHAN. But there is only one Templar in Jerusalem and he is my friend.

BROTHER. Who we are and the roles we are compelled to play are not always the same.

NATHAN. Well, friend or foe, let him do his worst – I will not rue a single day I have spent with Rachel.

I shall go and show this book to Saladin and there amaze them all.

BROTHER. God be with you. I should return to the Patriarch

NATHAN. But you have not seen her. You must come to us soon, and then come often. And maybe it's better if the Patriarch hears none of this yet. But then why not? No, tell him today, if you want.

BROTHER. He will hear nothing from me. God speed you.

NATHAN. Do not forget us, brother.

The BROTHER *is gone.*

My God, let me stand beneath the open sky. The dreadful knot that has so long entangled me is loosed. I have nothing in the world to hide and I am light. I can stand once more in the sight of men as freely as I do before you. You who alone need not judge us solely by our actions which are so seldom what we intended.

TEMPLAR.

TEMPLAR. Nathan

NATHAN. What are you doing here? I thought we were to meet at the Palace?

TEMPLAR. I've been already. I'm sorry. Don't be angry.

Would you mind my asking who left you just now?

NATHAN. Why? Do you know him?

TEMPLAR. It looked like the lay-brother the Patriarch uses for his dirty work

NATHAN. he's with the Patriarch, yes, but he's a good man

TEMPLAR. or that's the impression he likes to give. Did he say anything to you about me?

NATHAN. Not by name. But then perhaps he doesn't know your name

TEMPLAR. he doesn't

NATHAN. and it's true he did have something to say about an unnamed Templar

TEMPLAR. yes

NATHAN. but I don't think he can have meant you

TEMPLAR. why?

NATHAN. Because the Templar he spoke of had denounced me to the Patriarch

TEMPLAR. That's a lie. Listen to me, Nathan. I don't believe in retractions – what I've done, I've done. Which isn't to say I don't have regrets. But you know well enough what provoked me, what made my blood seethe. Yes, I'm an idiot. But I came here, body and soul ready to throw myself into your arms and you were so cold, not even cold, lukewarm, which is worse. So measured. I don't know how I managed to remain calm. That was the state I was in when Daya found me and whispered your secret. Well, it seemed the perfect explanation

NATHAN. did it

TEMPLAR. Let me finish. I imagined that having stolen her from a Christian you were determined not to lose her to one. I thought it was a good idea to put a knife to your throat

NATHAN. when you say good, in what sense are you using that word

TEMPLAR. Listen to me. So, I went to the Patriarch, but I didn't give him your name. I described the situation to him in general terms in order to get his opinion. Yes, it was stupid even to do that. But I didn't know what kind of man he was

NATHAN. and now

TEMPLAR. I've come to my senses. I want to try and put things right

NATHAN. how do you suggest doing that?

TEMPLAR. The Patriarch can only take her if she is yours alone

NATHAN. you may be right

TEMPLAR. so if you give her to me, he's powerless. I'd like to see him try to take my wife. Give her to me, Nathan. She's your daughter or she isn't, she's a Christian or a Jew, whatever. It doesn't matter to me. What is, is. Give her to me and I will never ask you about her for the rest of my life. We don't have much time.

NATHAN. You must think it's very important to me to keep the truth concealed?

TEMPLAR. I don't care what the truth is

NATHAN. in fact I've never, either to you or to anyone else who had the right to know, pretended that she was anything but a Christian and my adopted-daughter. Why I've never told Rachel is between me and her

TEMPLAR. and why tell her now? Why make her look on you with new eyes? Spare her. She is yours and all you need is her consent. Give her to me, I beg you. I can save her for you. Again. And I will.

NATHAN. You could have done, it's true. But not any more. It's too late.

TEMPLAR. How is it too late?

NATHAN. We have the Patriarch to thank for that.

TEMPLAR. The Patriarch doesn't matter

NATHAN. No, you see thanks to the Patriarch we know who her true family is

TEMPLAR. her true family

NATHAN. and now you must approach them and not me.

TEMPLAR. Poor Rachel, you're cursed where any other orphan would be blessed. Where are they?

NATHAN. Where are they?

TEMPLAR. And who are they?

NATHAN. A brother, in particular. He's the one you'd have to ask.

TEMPLAR. And what's he? A soldier? Priest?

NATHAN. I believe he's neither, or both. I'm not entirely sure

TEMPLAR. do you know anything else about him?

NATHAN. He's brave, apparently. And he'll take good care of Rachel

TEMPLAR. even if he is a Christian. How can you allow this, Nathan? How can you watch the pure wheat you've sown be choked with weeds? Does Rachel know any of this yet?

NATHAN. I don't know how she could. Where are you going?

TEMPLAR. To tell her. And see if she's the courage to make the only choice worthy of her

NATHAN. which is?

TEMPLAR. to follow me. Even if that means becoming the wife of a Muslim

NATHAN. a Muslim? How's that?

TEMPLAR. You'll see

NATHAN. Well you won't find her in there. She's with the Sultan's sister, Sittah

TEMPLAR. since when

NATHAN. and if you want to meet her brother, you should accompany me there.

TEMPLAR. Whose brother? Sittah's or Rachel's?

NATHAN. Maybe both.

    NATHAN *and* TEMPLAR *go*.

Eleven

Sittah's Harem. SITTAH *and* RACHEL.

SITTAH. I'm so pleased to meet you at last, my sweet. But don't look so worried. Or are you shy? Relax. Tell me all about yourself. Trust me.

RACHEL. Princess

SITTAH. please. Sittah. Your friend. Your sister.

Look at you, so young and clever and devout. I bet you've read everything

RACHEL. no, I haven't. I can hardly read at all

SITTAH. liar.

RACHEL. I've read a few things my father's written out for me, but I thought you meant books

SITTAH. I did

RACHEL. no, I've never tried to read a book

SITTAH. d'you really mean that

RACHEL. yes. My father hates that kind of learning from books which just crams the mind with dead ideas

SITTAH. so instead

RACHEL. he teaches me himself. Almost everything I know I can tell you where, how, why he taught me it.

SITTAH. He's a clever man your father

RACHEL. he is

SITTAH. What's the matter?

RACHEL. My father

SITTAH. You're crying

RACHEL. my father

I can't

SITTAH. Little one, what's happened? Rachel.

RACHEL. I'm going to lose him

SITTAH. who? Nathan. No, you shan't. I won't let it. Look at me: your sister gives you her word

RACHEL. you truly meant you'd be my sister

SITTAH. I did. I am. Now up you get, or I shall have to call someone.

RACHEL. I'm sorry. Forgive me. I forgot where I was, who you are.

SITTAH. Well, then

RACHEL. You must prevent it happening, sister. You must stop them trying to force another father on me.

SITTAH. Who wants to?

RACHEL. Daya. My good, bad Daya.

She took such care of me when I was child, you wouldn't believe it. She was my mother. And now she tortures me.

SITTAH. How?

RACHEL. Oh, it's done from love, I'm sure. But she's the kind of Christian who believes she alone knows the true path

SITTAH. I've met them

RACHEL. but now I've nothing left to fight her with

SITTAH. Tell me what she's done:

RACHEL. On our way here we passed a church – burnt out, the tower on the edge of falling. Daya stops, looks up and then at me. Her eyes are wet, she seems possessed. She grabs my hand and says 'Through here' and dives into the ruin. I am sure we will be crushed, something will fall on us. But then she stops again. We're stood before a blackened altar. She throws herself down at my feet, and wrings her hands and sobs

SITTAH. poor child

RACHEL. and with this terrifying look of love she pleads:
'Bow down and beg for mercy from the Virgin, for yourself
and for your family'.

Sittah, they were Christians. I was baptised. I am not
Nathan's daughter, he is not my father, oh God, he is not
my father.

SITTAH. Rachel, please, stand up. My brother's coming. Stand
up

Enter SALADIN.

SALADIN. What's the matter?

SITTAH. She is not herself

SALADIN. Who is it?

SITTAH. You know

SALADIN. Nathan's daughter?

What's happened to her?

SITTAH. Child, pull yourself together. The Sultan

RACHEL. no, I can't get up. Don't make me. I can't look him
in the face

SALADIN. Stand up

RACHEL. I can't look at him until he's promised me

SALADIN. whatever it is, you have my word

RACHEL. to let my father stay with me and me with him. I
don't know who it is who's claiming to be my real father
and I don't want to know. Is it blood that makes a father?
Blood and only blood?

SALADIN (*lifting her up*). I understand. What wicked person
gave you the idea that Nathan's not your father? Did they
have any proof? And if they did, no, fathers are not fathers
by blood alone, even amongst animals

Listen, Rachel, can I suggest something. These two fathers
warring over you – reject them both. And choose me. I'll be
your father.

SITTAH. Do it, Rachel. Do it.

SALADIN. I'd be a good father, the best. But wait, I've a better idea still. Not even the best father will stay around forever. What you need is someone who can run life's race beside you to the end. Yes? A friend. Am I right? Perhaps you have someone in mind.

SITTAH. You're making her blush

SALADIN. that was the idea. Blushing will make even an ugly face look pretty, and the pretty it makes radiant.

Because your father Nathan is outside with someone else. I wonder if you can guess

Sittah, may I?

SITTAH. Brother.

SALADIN *shows in* NATHAN *and* TEMPLAR.

SALADIN. My friends. Before we go any further, Nathan, I'm pleased to say that I no longer need your money

NATHAN. Sultan

SALADIN. the caravans have come and I'm richer than I've ever been. So now you must tell me what I can do for you: is there no great enterprise of yours I can support

NATHAN. please, I cannot give this my attention when there's a tearful eye that needs me to dry it.

NATHAN *goes to* RACHEL.

NATHAN. Why've you been crying? What's wrong? You're still my daughter, aren't you?

RACHEL. Yes, of course – but are you still my father

NATHAN. if you want me to be.

No more. We understand each other. Be cheerful. If your heart is still your own, no other loss can harm you, and your father will never be lost to you

RACHEL. that's the only thing that matters to me

TEMPLAR. the only thing

RACHEL. the only thing. I need nothing else

TEMPLAR. then I've been mistaken. Nathan, this changes everything.

Saladin, you summoned us here, but I've misled you. You no longer need trouble yourself with this. Forgive me

SALADIN. What's the matter now? Does everything always have to revolve around you?

TEMPLAR. You've heard what she said, you've seen them

SALADIN. I have. And it seems you weren't entirely certain of your facts

TEMPLAR. well now I am

SALADIN. Wait a moment, young man.

SALADIN *takes* RACHEL*'s hand.*

You mustn't pay too much attention to him. Or be too hard on him. If he wasn't the way he is, so hot-headed and red-blooded, then he might never have got around to saving you. You'll have to weigh the one against the other. Come on, put him to shame. Do what he ought to be doing, if he dared. Propose to him. If he rejects you, then at least you'll have the satisfaction of knowing who's the more courageous. What did he do for you after all? Got some smoke in his eyes? That's what my brother would have said. But I think maybe he has only Assad's shape and not his spirit. Come on.

SITTAH. Go on, Rachel. It's the least you can do to repay him

NATHAN. Saladin, Sittah, please wait

SALADIN. now it's you is it

NATHAN. there's someone else who needs to be consulted

SALADIN. who's denying that. No one would dare silence a foster-father who has done so much for her. Speak. You see I know all there is to know

NATHAN. Not quite all. It wasn't myself I meant. There is another. Someone you should meet before we proceed any further.

SALADIN. Who?

NATHAN. Rachel's brother.

RACHEL. I have a brother?

NATHAN. Yes

TEMPLAR. but where is he? I thought you said he'd be here

NATHAN. Have patience

TEMPLAR. first he forces a father on her, now he wants to foist a brother too

SALADIN. that is beneath you, Christian. My brother would never have uttered such stupidity.

NATHAN. Forgive him. I can. Who knows what we would have thought in his place, at his age.

(*To* TEMPLAR.) Of course, my friend, suspicion quickly flames into distrust. But if you'd only let me know your true name

TEMPLAR. What do you mean?

NATHAN. You are not Conrad von Stauffen

TEMPLAR. then who am I?

NATHAN. Leo Vilnek

TEMPLAR. am I

NATHAN. oh, I don't deny you may have some right to the other name as well

TEMPLAR. I believe I do

NATHAN. your mother's name was Stauffen. But Conrad was not your father, he was your mother's brother.

TEMPLAR. How do you know that?

NATHAN. Because your real father was my friend

TEMPLAR. I don't see how that's possible

NATHAN. he called himself Wolf, but he was not German. He had met your mother here, before I knew him. She was

German, and they moved to Swabia where you were born.
But persecution drove them into exile. So they returned, to
this land of exiles, where I met them.

TEMPLAR. But what has this to do with Rachel's brother?

NATHAN. You, their son they must have left in Swabia, in the
care of your uncle Conrad, a Knight Templar

TEMPLAR. Enough. Tell me where Rachel's brother is

NATHAN. he is standing before me now.

TEMPLAR. What are you saying

NATHAN. that you are Rachel's brother

TEMPLAR. me

RACHEL. my brother

SITTAH. brother and sister

NATHAN. your mother died giving birth to a daughter, whom
your father could not care for. So he entrusted her to his
closest friend, a Jew.

RACHEL. My brother

TEMPLAR. No. She is not my sister. She can't be.

RACHEL (*to* NATHAN). Then it can't be true. Not if he
doesn't feel it. It isn't true.

SALADIN. No, it's simply that there's no truth in him. He's an
imposter. The face, the voice, none of it belongs to him.
He's fake. Unless you can acknowledge her.

TEMPLAR. Please, Sultan, you can never have seen Assad in
a moment like this. Please don't misjudge both him and me.

Nathan, you give and you take away. No, you have given
me infinitely more than you have taken. A sister. My sister.

TEMPLAR *embraces* RACHEL.

TEMPLAR. Rachel

NATHAN. you must call her Lena

RACHEL. No. I am your Rachel. You cannot disown me now

NATHAN. nor do I. You can both be my children. If you want. Why shouldn't my daughter's brother be my son?

They embrace.

SALADIN (*to* SITTAH). What are you thinking, sister?

SITTAH. It moves me

SALADIN. and I tremble at the thought of what may be to come. Prepare yourself

SITTAH. what for?

SALADIN. Nathan, a word.

Did you say

NATHAN. what

SALADIN. I can hardly dare to ask it. Her father wasn't born in Germany, he wasn't German by birth

NATHAN. no

SALADIN. what was he then? Where did he come from?

NATHAN. He would never tell me. I asked him but

SALADIN. he wasn't a Westerner, a European

NATHAN. no, that much he did admit. His first language was Persian

SALADIN. it's him. I know it. It was him

NATHAN. who?

SALADIN. My brother. Assad. It can only have been.

NATHAN. If you believe so, this book may be your confirmation.

NATHAN gives SALADIN the breviary.

NATHAN. Here he wrote his family tree.

SALADIN. So my brother, that was where you rode out to.

NATHAN. They know nothing of this. You must decide how much you wish to tell them.

SALADIN. How can I not acknowledge my own brother's children? My nephew. My niece. My children. D'you think I'm going to let you have them to yourself?

(*Out loud.*) Sittah. It's them.

The lost children of our lost brother. You are home.

SALADIN *embraces them.*

SITTAH. How could it be otherwise?

SITTAH *embraces them.*

SALADIN (*to* TEMPLAR). And now you young man, will have to show me some respect. And love.

(*to* RACHEL.) And to you, my daughter, I promised I would be the prince of fathers, and I shall

SITTAH. And you must still call me sister, and not aunt.

SALADIN. My son. My Assad. My lost Assad's son.

TEMPLAR. I am of your blood. These were the stories they told me as a child, which filled my dreams. And which I never dared believe.

SALADIN. Look at him. The rascal knew this all along, and yet he would have let me murder him. You wait.

They continue to embrace in silence.

End.